When Christians Retire

Finding New Purpose in Your Bonus Years

Dwight Hervey Small

Beacon Hill Press of Kansas City
Kansas City, Missouri

Copyright 2000
by Beacon Hill Press of Kansas City

ISBN 083-411-8386

Printed in the
United States of America

Cover Design: Michael Walsh

Library of Congress Cataloging-in-Publication Data

Small, Dwight Hervey.
  When Christians retire: finding new purpose in your bonus years / Dwight Hervey Small.
      p. cm.
  Includes bibliographical references.
  ISBN 0-8341-1838-6 (pb)
    1. Retirees—Religious life. 2. Retirement—Religious aspects—Christianity. I. Title.

  BV4596.R47 S65 2000
  248.8'5—dc21

                                                    00-046803

10   9   8   7   6   5   4   3   2   1

Contents

Introduction   5

1   Adjusting to a New Role   7

2   Finding My New Identity   19

3   Overcoming Losses   39

4   Letting Go and Moving On   57

5   Discovering New People and New Roles   69

6   Feeling Unfinished and Unfulfilled   105

7   Keeping Eternity's Values in View   121

Notes   137

Select Bibliography   141

Introduction

Dear Mr. Small,

I've read several of your books, and I know you are a retired Christian sociologist. I have a problem. I retired recently, and I'm going through the identity thing. I'm really confused about who I am now and what I should do with my life. Golf, gardening, and a bit of travel isn't enough. I'm often depressed, and would like my life to count for something more. Do you have any suggestions?

Alex Comfort may have had this oft-repeated dilemma in mind when he commented, "Two weeks is about the ideal length of time to retire."[1] Ask anyone now retired, especially those from professional or business careers, and most will agree. Their reply usually reflects some difficulty or disappointment in a lack of direction or an inability to find fulfillment in this new beginning. More than anything else, what they are saying—whether they recognize it or not—is that life needs to be meaningful and significant for retirement to have real value.

University of California historian Page Smith goes so far as to oppose retirement altogether, insisting that retirement leaves us at loose ends and underfoot, contributing only to the "hardening of arteries, joints, and opinions."[2]

But can the value of retirement years be dismissed so easily? No. The brighter side—a newly productive and satisfying life for God and one's self, a life that counts retirement years as bonus years—is what this book is all about.

There are effective solutions to the psychological and social needs that make for a positive outlook. We need to face the serious problems that retirement dislocations can force upon us. Retirement can be either *dream* or *disaster*. So let's begin with the most difficult of transitional adjustments, find the means for coping, then turn to the excellent possibilities ahead. Let me say it loudly and clearly—God has a retirement plan for each of us—for *you!* And He waits to make it known! It is ours to pray about, actively seek, and then commit to.

As a personal note, I highly recommend your reading Jules Z. Willing's *The Reality of Retirement,* a secular book with a lot of practical wisdom.

1

Adjusting to a New Role

Retirement: This new "land of the forever liberated." You're on your own now. It's free sailing ahead. But wait, are you sure of your destination?

It's a radical change—the kind of shock that has little cushioning. Men and women of varied backgrounds are often deeply troubled by retirement adjustments and are vulnerable to distressing episodes while making the social and psychological adjustments in retirement's crossover process.

All-Too-Typical Scenarios

When you retire and the long-anticipated day of closure arrives, the envisioned venture ahead is briefly obscured by the nostalgia that inevitably occurs when separating from a long career. Although essentially euphoric, suddenly you are fighting moist eyes and a lump in the throat. Desk drawers have to be emptied, files must be cleaned out, and a mountain of memorabilia is carefully boxed up or casually thrown out. Another vision has taken over. In this transition you are understandably a bit numb. You haven't been this way before. And if you're married, there are adjustments rising on the home front as well.

For one last time, the door is locked. With contrived casualness, you repeat good-byes for the second or third time. With less notice than expected, you just walk away from it all. Your associates may steal side-glances, but no one steps up to stop the action; there's nothing to stop, nothing more to say. This is it! This is retirement!

Taking the first untested steps, you have joined the ranks of "retiree." Perhaps a celebration party will break the awkwardness the first evening, but more likely you'll have a quiet dinner with your spouse and a few friends. It hardly seems real. However ceremoniously, let's face it, a lifetime of good years is over, ended abruptly with little more than a smile and a wave.

For so long you said, "Can't wait for the new life to begin!" Why then a sudden surge of turbulent, ambivalent feelings? In ways you couldn't have imagined just weeks before, your self-affirming status has begun to erode. Personal self-definition isn't that clear any more, and like an adolescent you might ask, "Who *am* I?" Watch out, because you could be hit by one enormous change in status and a diminishing self-valuation. Your life is becoming something like a vacuum, and it doesn't run by your watch like it used to!

New-Life Characteristics

So is it "freedom at last," where there are no more time demands and it's a free lifestyle of leisure galore? One thing seems sure: the work routine has disappeared. It's the chance to live those long-held dreams, the opportunity to do "all the things I've wanted to do but never had time for."

Exactly what is so promising about retirement? There's no contract that spells out the details, no blueprint that seems to fit everyone. So how do we know what to expect? What if gains do not outweigh losses? What about psychological costs down the road? What about major social adjustments? Can we handle it all without some mental turmoil? What are your own hopes and dreams? And more importantly, around what center will your life be organized? Is there productive life after a career ends? If so, of what kind? How should you restructure your new world? And what about *Christian* retirees in particular? Are adjustments different from the general population? Do Christians have prospects and ongoing life-purposes unlike those of non-Christians?

Successive Life-Stages

In the mid-70s, Gail Sheehy popularized the term "passages" in a book based on a 10-year study by a team led by Daniel Levinson. Levinson's own book was titled *The Seasons of a Man's Life.* Twenty years later, Sheehy's newer book on this subject is titled *New Passages.*

Today we speak of the "seasons" of life and of "passages" between them. In some instances both spouses retire at the same time, and that calls for a whole new set of compromises and adjustments. Tasks of major proportions immediately lie ahead for both partners. One challenge is the call for wise and mature marital negotiation.

A helpful study is William Bridges's book *Transitions: Making Sense of Life's Changes.* In introducing the theme he gives substance to the lines of T. S. Eliot in "Little Gidding": "What we call the beginning is often the end, and to make an end is to make a beginning. The end is where we start from."[1] Bridges elaborates on the idea that you not begin any new phase of life without first closing off and leaving behind many primary attachments and commitments. The transition follows a four-step progression:

(1) *Closure with the Past*

As you leave the network of associates you've known intimately in the working world, this network must be replaced with a new, equally significant group of people. Otherwise, you may suffer a painful and debilitating reaction to the loss. Before the void can be filled with new people, however, there must be a sense of closure with former relationships, opening the way to accepting and building new ones. Bridges's word is *detachment*—separation from yesterday's social network, the all-important first step I choose to call *closure*.

(2) *Repositioning*

People in social systems are organized in hierarchies, each having position and rank (the so-called pecking order). Your place in the hierarchy tells everyone who you are in the organization and where you belong in the social ranking. Primary attachments are comprised of the group of people with whom you work and includes every person and activity that makes up the organizational structure. When you retire, you undergo change in position, status, and rank. New skills have to be acquired to ensure that the replacement group of people meets with equal acceptability. "Repositioning" takes place only when there has been *(a)* closure with past status and position, and *(b)* separation from the former network of associates.

(3) *Reorientation*

As we orient ourselves around our careers, this process becomes the means by which we measure the progress of our lives. When we retire we must reorient ourselves, first away from those careers to which we've been so intimately oriented for so long. No longer is career a useful measure to define our lives. In turn, we reorient around a new status, new self-definition, new roles—all to fit the new situation. The occasion for this is retirement, which in the lifetime of most persons is the last rite of passage.

(4) *Confirming New Realities*

We can no longer *confirm* the past as a present reality but need now to *confirm new realities,* exchanging the old for the new. Here we begin to deal with our situation deliberately and realistically. We *disconfirm,* or take a position that's against our tendency not to accept. In fact, we disconfirm our tendency to idealize either the past or the future. This deliberate intention paves the way for realistically moving into present time without being bound by psychological past-tense shackles.

When we progress through any major life-transition, *endings always come before beginnings.* For some individuals, these transitions are apparently unexceptional—no special concerns are associated with disconfirming the past and confirming the present—no big deal, as we say. For others the transition is painfully exceptional—totally disruptive, even to the point of bringing on a brief state of deep depression and dysfunction. Of course, the transition does not incorporate identical hurdles for every person. Different degrees of difficulty are to be expected and treated accordingly.

Bridging Between Life-Stages

Transition bridges are the movement between any two distinct stages of life. It involves moving out of one stage marked by stability and certainty, then briefly passing through a period of change, loss, uncertainty, and instability. Becoming reestablished in the new stage is once again marked by relative stability and certainty. It isn't possible to straddle two stages at the same time, but there is a brief occupation of an unfamiliar, untested neutral zone with disturbing uncertainty, confusion, ambiguity, and instability.

Since individuals and circumstances differ widely, the degree of difficulty accompanying the passage cannot be accurately predicted. There is no way to tell which elements will be easiest, which more unsettling. The older a person becomes, the more defined and concrete their indi-

viduality. This usually reaches a high point around retirement age.

In the bridging process we "reposition" ourselves by
taking our place as permanent exiles from the past, having
moved away from the workday world where formerly we
spent most of our waking hours. We move first into the
neutral zone, no longer living intermittently in two different
worlds—the career world with workplace associates and
the private world of family and friends. No longer do we
experience the rhythm of this dual existence involving both
worlds. As Jules Willing puts it, we "move completely into
the smaller quarters of our private life."[2]

The Status That Defines Us

Stepping into retirement is stepping into an entirely different universe with a lifestyle all its own. Your personal
psychological equilibrium becomes upset and certain familiar supports are swept away. Hopefully, a spouse or close
friend becomes a support system. Different situations call
for different support persons, so trust God for His choice.

The Transition

Retirement is the final adult transition in which we can
measure how well people adapt to leaving the attachments
of a former stage and taking up attachments in a succeeding one. We want to know how others have fared in conditions similar to those we ourselves might encounter. In a
later chapter we will take up the transition to eternity, re-
viewing the Christian's anticipation of the last earthly move
and the prospect God has given us in Christ. Preparation
for eternity is in fact a major part of the equation for successful Christian retirement, the necessary underpinning of
everything else. How we look upon that last transition will
affect how we plan for the years of retirement.

No Longer Indispensable

Perhaps the hardest thing for you to swallow is the realization that no matter what your position was in the world of work, you are no longer the indispensable individual with long-term, rock-solid, taken-for-granted recognition among working associates. On your first visit back to the workplace, you'll most likely hear, "We're getting along just fine, thank you!" So the first casualty is status, recognition, a former sense of place, and self-assured identity. These invariably fade and are no longer viable gateways as before.

Harder to swallow, as Jules Willing points out, is realization that your contributions to the professional, business, or common work world—contributions once gratefully credited to you—are no longer important to anyone besides you. It doesn't matter how significant contributions might have been at the time, it's all surpassed by new challenges, new methods and solutions, new advances—all credited to new people you might not even know. The value of what you worked so hard to accomplish is diminished in the light of swiftly moving changes, and having your contributions devalued is to *feel your very self devalued!*

Just when your self-esteem needs to be shored up by recognition of what you've contributed, those accomplishments lose their significance. We forget that those who preceded us felt the same loss when they moved on. "It is" says Willing, "as though one's contribution has been canceled from history."[3] James Thomson of the University of Nebraska put it in a nutshell with his comment that retirement adjustment may be easier if one is a "never was" than a "has been."

Changing Role of Work

Retirement is about self-occupation. Like former vocations it involves what you do with time, talent, and energy alongside those who continue with full-time jobs. It takes preparation and dedication if self-occupation is to be productive and rewarding. This requires a much closer integration of occupation and leisure, a more relaxed occupational life.

Self-occupation for retirees involves:

(1) adoption of a purpose and finding the occupations to fulfill it.

(2) preparation to fulfill needs and opportunities newly discovered.

(3) dedication to the required tasks and energy to pursue them with enthusiasm.

(4) anticipation of the benefits and rewards of the occupational activity.

At this stage of life, a freely chosen occupation should be entered with carefully thought-through purposes that are taken on with a definite commitment. The new freedom to choose for yourself is refreshing and involves learning to live with less highly structured work conditions, less tightly scheduled days. If leisure living is not to be ill-spent, it must be measured in terms of the fulfillment of worthy purposes.

Tracing the Steps

Part of adapting to the new status of retirement is the importance of this changing role of work. In retirement there is an abrupt reduction of official involvement and with it loss of prominence and authority. Retirement forces us to understand that work now takes on a whole new meaning. Among other things, relationships hold an entirely different power equation.

In retirement your self-esteem may be lessened. Because the use of former talents is greatly reduced if not eliminated altogether, the transition to lesser status and recognition tends to be detrimental to maintaining a sense of self-worth. Just when you become happily retired, you realize all that went into the years spent getting an education, advancing in a career, honing abilities to manage life around you. A whole way of life had been carved out around the skills that brought opportunities for advancement along with increasing responsibilities and rewards.

But now it's easy to question your purpose in retirement. Do your most serious decisions from now on involve whether to play a round of golf, putter in the garden, watch TV, or relax with the latest novel? Don't give in to a big letdown or romanticize this retirement thing! You can make life count for something real.

Setting Goals

We must realize the reestablishment of goals for the new life, but not all retirees face the same problems. My personal struggle was to accept irreversible change and irretrievable loss, factors very common in retirement. Accepting that change and loss without mentally turning back is the biggest challenge.

One executive put it this way: "All I've got left is my future!" Another remarked, "I feel like I'm a missing person waiting to be found." A third wistfully quipped, "Ah, yes, I have a wonderful future behind me!" And from still another, "It's not exactly a picnic, this retirement thing!" We need to know which strategies to adopt if we're to turn a difficult transition into a skillful resolution.

Ensuring Successful Passage

A successful passage entails seeing the years ahead as part of the entire continuum of your life, a living extension of the past that bridges what's left behind. In anticipation of the transition, you can attempt to learn everything possi-

ble about goals and potential opportunities, planning whatever seems to match your hopes for the remaining years
and, most importantly, what will bring a sense of fulfilling
God's highest purposes. Not every goal is a visible one.

The very core meaning of transition is "moving *from*
something *to* something." It's the "to something" that's often
unclear and not well prepared for. What seems to be a suit-
able option, even though carefully chosen, might turn out
differently than anticipated and require another decision.

Retirement often begins with false starts. While momentarily frustrating, this is no permanent obstacle. Experi-
menting may prove to be a good thing. It is wise to look at
the transition early and as realistically as possible.

If we're not to be blindsided by this major status
change and its extensive realignment of life, we need to
know as accurately as possible what positive end we're
moving toward and how to make the best choices. In this
regard, it is worthwhile to talk with individuals who have
made the passage happily, evaluating how they are getting
along in their new circumstances. Assessing another couple
should include knowledge of what their life was like before
as well as what it is now. In this fashion they may be helpful by indicating both positive and negative factors as well
as how they've coped with certain problems. Find out what
issues they still face. It is critical for each of us to define
our core self, but it is imperative to consider every factor
that makes for a new and satisfying self-definition.

> *Lord, give me faith to live from day to day,*
> *With tranquil heart to do my simple part,*
> *And, with hand in Thine, just go Thy way.*
> *Lord, give me faith! To trust, if not to know;*
> *With quiet mind in all things Thee to find,*
> *And, childlike, go where Thou wouldst have me go.*

Lord, give me faith! to leave it all with Thee.
The future is Thy gift, I would not lift
The veil Thy love has hung 'twixt it and me.

—John Oxenham[4]

2

Finding My New Identity

Coming on a crash scene is a shocking experience—being in one is far worse. The same is true when the doctor brings the news of a potentially debilitating, possibly fatal illness. The questions are the same. What course of events can we expect? Will we still be functional? What does the future hold? What are the costs? These are retirement questions as well.

The difficult transition many retirees experience is illustrated by what I know best, my own brief but traumatic episode of depression over the "loss of place" following retirement. It was a crash scene—nonfatal but critical, a "delayed postretirement disorientation." Such psychological downers are sometimes referred to as "crossover crises."

My early years of retirement began as a time of celebrating "The Grand Release." I was free from obligatory work schedules and could engage in projects that suited my interests and our interests as a couple. It also involved a major move that enabled us to return to a beloved circle of old friends in San Jose, California.

Initial interests made for an exciting start-up. However, the move was not everything we'd dreamed. We had idealized retirement as a relaxed, nondemanding "do what we always wanted to do" time. In the euphoria, it hardly seemed that we would soon need to find a more fulfilling goal. Nor did I dream that the professional life I was leaving had been the basis of my self-identity. Retirement would require major adjustments.

At age 62, I left a much-loved college professorship, preceded by years of happy, fruitful pastorates. Severe vision problems related to years of diabetes dictated early retirement, although the vision problem was later resolved at a famous retinal clinic.

Like so many men intensely active throughout their professional or business careers, *what I was as a person equated with what I did.* Day by day, week by week, year in and year out, my self-image had built on the goals of a productive life, much like my peers in secular achievement-oriented careers—just typical male professional development. Nothing about this ever seemed in the least unspiritual. I had genuinely desired to be God's man and the servant of others, not calling attention to myself or my ministry. Nonetheless, subconsciously there was that all-too-human desire to make some mark in life (mind you, "some mark *for God*"!).

Once retired, all that remained when the newness wore off was the occupation I had brought with me—my writing, which I regarded as ministry. I assumed this would fill my life, along with socializing with old friends. Additionally, I would surely be teaching a Bible class, satisfying the need to be ministering within a fellowship. Not once did Ruth and I entertain the thought of moving again. But within three years we returned to the central coast of California, a decision made within a short period of time and for reasons only partially compelling. We settled in Santa Maria, near our children and grandchildren, and not far from Ruth's sister and her husband. The housing market was reasonable, and the small city seemed attractive.

But then, increasingly bored after three years in Santa Maria, I approached my former colleague at Westmont College with the idea of a coauthored research and writing project. This resulted in a large project that consumed three years and resulted in a technical book that found its way into a number of university law libraries. It kept me extremely busy but also housebound and socially inactive.

The delight of this second relocation was that it allowed my occasional return to the campus for library research and enjoyable visits with former faculty friends. I could walk the same beautiful hilly paths and envision myself still functioning as part of the academic community. On those occasions my retirement didn't seem so final. But that bordered on denial.

Within a couple of years I didn't feel like driving the distance to campus. Health problems made walking the campus hills less easy. By every practical measure, life was being tied ever more closely to home and the requirements of my new world. The fantasy of living in two worlds was short-lived.

In reality, most of my days and weeks were spent at home in my study with few personal contacts other than a couple of fine neighbors and the once-a-week friends at church. The developing lifestyle was hardly satisfying to the social person my professional life had trained me to be. Little did I realize that two relocations in three years had added to the serious discontinuity and general destabilization of my life.

Here I was—no longer a professor, counselor, or familiar campus figure. No longer was I making important decisions on the Faculty Senate. Rarely did I speak at conferences or preach on Sundays as in years past. Invariably I found myself talking in the past tense—who I'd been, what I'd done, people I'd known.

The pendulum swung in the opposite direction as I said no to speaking engagements, seminars, conferences—even to church commitments. By deliberate choice, I removed myself from opportunities and obligations. After all, I tried to convince myself, hadn't I given years to all these things? But I was building a wall between me and vital life in the community.

Delayed Postretirement Syndrome

The problem continued. Social life was largely limited and six years into retirement—three years after moving to our second location—I began to question every aspect of this less-than-fulfilling new lifestyle. *"Should I ever have fully retired? Who am I now? Who should I be? What meaningful occupations should I be engaged in? Is there any new purpose I can fulfill? Am I really out-to-pasture but unwilling to face it? Do I resent my writing ministry somewhat because it confines me to this house?"* Things were beginning to come apart. I knew it; Ruth knew it.

It was an increasingly uneasy time. Instead of taking a corrective course, I simply dug in and nursed negative attitudes. In these early stages I didn't realize that increasing restlessness might suddenly erupt into full-fledged depression as well as a form of dysfunction. I, of all people, was too strong to succumb to anything like depression or dysfunction, I thought. Ruth, however, could sense something ominous was taking place. She prayed much and hid an anxious heart.

My history evidenced no episodes of psychological disorder, no seriously acute periods of extreme anxiety. I simply had not considered the effects of an abrupt transition with its altered set of established roles and routines. I was victimized by something completely unexpected. Without warning I was helpless to cope with ordinary routines and emotions. Such a state can only be described as "delayed postretirement disorientation syndrome accompanied by depression and dysfunction."

We understand dysfunction to be the inability to project normal daily objectives and get on with them, an inability to organize accustomed tasks. For me there was also a strange disengagement from organized patterns of thought and action. I was gripped by a hope-negating mentality that I did not understand, could not cope with, or escape. Present time appeared devoid of purpose, future time without positive prospects. Daily life, dominated by insecurity and uncertainty, had come to a virtual standstill. It seemed that everything was closing in—a frightening and foreboding sense of confinement. Everything about my life had seriously narrowed, bringing me to this sense of depressive entrapment.

To magnify my problem, we had just returned from two very special visits, with old friends who had retired. We'd all been close friends since seminary days. In retirement both men were now continuing as half-time associates in large city churches. With the best of two worlds, they were able to enjoy half their time with ministry and half with family life, friends, and leisure activities—a beautiful balance. Both couples were finding fulfillment as they continued serving the Lord but in less strenuous capacities. As both couples continued to live in the same homes as before, there was no dislocation, no upheaval of any kind. Life went on much the same with no major discontinuity. Friends and family were nearby. There was no reason to compare past with present. Retirement held few evidences of a different life, as nearly every meaningful activity and relationship remained the same. Even status and role performance was little changed.

As I compared my own dislocations and present lack of fulfillment, a severe reaction set in. Deep inside I envied these men and their active, though lower-key, positions!

They'd made it; I hadn't. Why hadn't I planned better? Or differently? Now I'm locked into my own lack of fore-thought! Where do I go from here? How badly this centered on "I . . . I . . . I, me . . . me . . . me."

Returning home from the second of these visits, I experienced an unusual resistance to entering our house. Once inside I had no inclination to go to my study. The very room seemed forbidding. Everything symbolized isolation and disconnectedness. It was all starting to reach desperate proportions.

Over the next eight days—the most trying period of my adult years—there stretched an acute episode of disorientation, depression, and dysfunction. Often during the night hours I would waken to morbid thoughts and severe nervous tension, sometimes in a cold sweat. Even at such unearthly hours I wanted to get out of the house, to flee "the problem" as it were.

It was all highly irrational, yet even recognizing the absurdity of my reactions only added to the problem, for then I felt ashamed and guilty to be subject to such distortions of reality, such incompetence to rectify my situation. Most troubling of all was pondering how a mature Christian could be captive to such gripping fears and experience such disabling depression. For years I had genuinely helped others resolve what was now beyond resolving for myself.

Thankfully, I'd not lost awareness of the Lord's grace and goodness or His promise never to leave or forsake me. I was clinging to Rom. 8:28: "For we know that in everything God works for good with those who love him, who are called according to his purpose." But, wait, maybe I didn't fit the promise at this time for some reason? Doubts crept in over scriptural promises. Completely nontypical, this condition was nevertheless very real.

The downturn continued unrelentingly and with increasing severity. Able to sleep only a few hours each night, I was continually tired, and the loss of energy pulled me down further. On occasion I would rise well before dawn and seek the Lord's face, pleading with Him to deliver me from this darkness of spirit, this absence of direction, this crippling emotional weakness. Often He met me, but over-all I was losing the battle. I'd never known such insecurity as this. A classic cry became mine:

> *Come down, O Christ, and help me!*
> *Reach out Thy hand!*
> *I'm drowning on a stormier sea*
> *Than Simon on Thy Galilee!*
> —Oscar Wilde, "E. Tenebris"

Intermittently through the days of that agonizing week, hopeful moments would return, but all too briefly. Classic hymns had a magnificent power to temporarily lift me out of myself and into God's presence—yet again, only tem-porarily. When I was unable to pray with my own words, I would pray the verses of relevant hymns, second only to Scripture in providing what sustaining strength I received each day. The glorious vision of God contained therein led me upward with affirmations of His love and the liberating grace of Christ my Lord. I knew that underneath were the everlasting arms! Thankfully, I never lost sight of that. But as yet this wasn't victory.

Continually the conviction grew that God had His rea-sons for permitting this affliction of mind and spirit. I was beginning to recognize there would be no final deliverance until certain lessons had been learned, certain recommit-ments made. Clearly, there was *His* part and there was *my* part. Deliverance couldn't come without first a searching of heart and life and a releasing of all my concerns into His hands. Neither could I afford to forever look back; the answer wasn't in the past. In quiet desperation I clung to the clear impression that God had good purposes in it all. But at the time nothing seemed clear.

Early on, a journal of those successive days and nights began to take shape (a writer's impulse, no doubt). I had no conscious purpose other than a continuous reminder of what I was going through and the nature of the struggle. Then as time went on, those accumulating insights served as a powerful testimony to progress being made into the light and strength of His grace. This was encouraging evidence of the special times when He did break through with precious assurances—even when progress was small and uneven. The journal was also a strong testament to His gift of increasing self-understanding. Later it proved useful as I pondered how to more precisely relate this experience in book form and share my journey with fellow Christian retirees. But most importantly, I knew that He was there—*there for me!*

As the days multiplied, there were more insights, more assurances, renewed inner strength. Nonetheless, toward the end of that black week the progress was overwhelmed by a terribly regressive setback, as though the enemy had gotten the upper hand. I began to cry out to God to defeat his strategies, claiming the promise, "Greater is He that is in you than he that is in the world." I felt I was actually snatching defeat from victory, as it were—losing the battle.

God's Special Partners

I found I could not—indeed need not—go through this ordeal alone. Leaning on my own resources, I was sinking. With a twist of irony, I asked myself "Who is the pastor's pastor, the counselor's counselor? Who can minister to me at this time?"

One morning about 4:30 I awakened Ruth, asking her just to sit, talk, read Scripture, and pray with me. I could only sob out my feelings of helplessness and try to describe the sense of isolation and surrounding darkness. I feared a hopeless future if I were no longer able to be a healthy, ministering person. Though a child of God, I had become filled with irrational fears and morbid thoughts, making me ashamed and guilt-ridden that somehow these disabilities would hamper my Christian walk.

In her own wonderful way, Ruth was there with me and for me. Shining through was the understanding of accumulated years of companionship and sharing. Intuitively, she knew how to facilitate my need for self-understanding through listening, caring comments, biblical insights, and positive encouragement.

Little did I realize how severely this crisis of mine touched her spirit with an equal depth of anguish. In the midst of depression I became self-focused. Every caring spouse in such circumstances must recognize this and patiently work around it.

About three years prior to this, we had renewed a friendship with a dear couple—a retired minister and his wife.

They were living a short 35 miles away, and our fellowship resumed in what quickly became a more intimate, blessed relationship. I could not have known then that the ministry of this caring friend would be needed in a time of crisis in my life.

Together the four of us found ourselves mutually supported by happy times. But now in this crisis a critical test of that relationship was soon to come. Could he be "the pastor's pastor, the counselor's counselor?"

Eight days into this darkness, I felt compelled to give T. G. an early morning call. From my rather broken speech with its emotional overtones he could readily sense my need was critical. So with a pastor's intuition, he and his wife went to prayer. Soon after breakfast Ruth and I were on our way to their condo.

Wisely, the two wives left us for most of the day. For T. G. and me, it was a blessed time of deep relating, washed with tears and lifted by prayer, infused with unspoken mutual understanding and empathy. Together we stood upon God's Word as the Spirit of God brought relevant promises to mind.

Is any support greater than that of dear ones—family or friends—who can stand with us and be part of the battle? But make no mistake; they, too, suffer with us. And when victory comes, theirs is also a share in the rejoicing. Is this not the mutual burden-bearing of which the New Testament speaks (Gal. 6:2)? How true is the word of Jesus that burdens become lighter when laid upon Him. He is our true Yokefellow while others share as well. Here the divine and the human team together.

That day spent with T. G. was the turning point. Beyond all doubt! The clouds broke, and the sun shone within my spirit once again! Within a few days I was back to normal inner health and with new-found self-understanding. God had met me. Deeply meaningful lessons were falling into place. To hear what He was saying, to see what He was doing, was encouraging, yes, downright exciting.

Recovered!

Over the next few months, only a few minor setbacks dogged my steps, then full recovery. Best of all, throughout that recovery period, I knew the battle was over, the victory won. I simply had to lay hold of it, then live out its reality, as God measured out His strength on a day-to-day basis. How blessed was Caroline V. Sandell-Berg's beautiful Swedish hymn:

> *Day by day, and with each passing moment,*
>   *Strength I find to meet my trials here.*
> *Trusting in my Father's wise bestowment,*
>   *I've no cause for worry or for fear.*
> *He whose heart is kind beyond all measure*
>   *Gives unto each day what He deems best*
> *Lovingly, its part of pain and pleasure*
>   *Mingling toil with peace and rest.*

I had allowed life to turn inward. I had built a wall around myself that exacerbated the fundamental problem, a wall that *closed me into myself* and *closed me out* of any possible usefulness. Consequently, I lost perspective. It was self-imposed confinement of the spirit. Of this, my study and the house were symbolic. I had managed to isolate and insulate myself, the problem being largely of my own making. Positively, this meant the solution was also largely of my own making although, of course, not without His intervention and help. This is where retirees in the same situation need to be honest with themselves and ask, "How have I contributed to the problem?" It wasn't easy to admit *"I'm the problem."*

Having turned away from opportunities for ministry, I had locked myself in my little writing world inhabited by a word processor and a bookish project. Failing to cultivate friends locally, I also brushed off social occasions that could have been helpful both to me and to Ruth. At times— and for shame—I "just couldn't be bothered" and so was paying the price. Eventually God got through and assured me of His purposes for me—*if* I would accept them as His best and my best. He asked, "Will you turn everything over to Me? There's nothing I cannot handle, you know."

"Yes, Lord, I agree; I submit. I'm ready to comply. Only You must help me."

Painful as it was, the message was getting through. There

was indeed hope for a fulfilling life ahead, perhaps more just *growing* than *doing*. His proposition was one that only faith could grasp. But obedience required letting Him take greater control and trusting Him in the dark as in the light.

At just the right juncture, Ruth said, "The Lord's given me a verse for you: Jer. 29:11, 'For I know the plans I have for you, says the LORD, plans for welfare and not for evil, to give you a future and a hope.'" She added the observation that nothing in that promise points to the past; the past is no longer relevant. It's the present.

So Ruth and I together claimed this promise for ourselves. There was a future and a hope! It included both of us. Indeed! It lay in God's sovereign will! I could trust Him and rest at peace in that divine will! The price? No more leaning on self-assertive, anxious planning of my own.

In practical terms, rectifying the situation began when I took steps to correct my isolation from all ministering opportunities. I began by doing some volunteer counseling at the church. I could quickly say yes when God revealed a need He wanted to fill through me, however small it might seem. Moreover, I'm content now to rest in the fact that He is the One, not I, who both opens doors and closes them! How releasing is this dependence on Him to cancel out nagging anxieties! What joy and freedom!

Subsequently, He's led me to occasional speaking and teaching engagements and individuals who need counseling. For example the young pastor overburdened and needing to get away, but unable to do so unless I offered to preach in his place without honorarium. There are many needs out there if we but have eyes to see them and willingness to meet them.

Subsequent to all this, I found a particular fellowship of wounded saints—*pastors*. This became clear recently when I led a church seminar in the vicinity of a Christian retirement center where a number of pastors reside. I told my story and pastors were among those who sought to talk to me afterward. ("If *Dwight* could bare his soul, maybe *I* can too.") Clearly, these problems are very real and exist wherever retirees are found.

Understand this, my retired Christian friend, experienced ministering persons also must learn to be available to God on a day-to-day basis. This is what God requires first—not *all* He requires, but what He *first* requires. Thus, it is not our task to devise *His* purposes or arrange *His* plans for Him.

I needed a greater desire to have Him structure my days, programing things as He sees fit. With a new attitude of positive expectation, I found the fresh experience of His faithfulness. But there were areas that needed to be turned over, attitudes that needed to be dealt with—a continuous process of recognizing His hand and gladly submitting.

This was not *resignation,* but rather *affirmation!* Recall the lines in Frances R. Havergal's hymn "Like a River Glorious":

We may trust Him fully All for us to do;
They who trust Him wholly Find Him wholly true.

I'm persuaded there is indeed "life after retirement" to those who seek His leading and empowering. There are opportunities for "creative usefulness," even when your circle of influence is limited. He wants us to be His partners just where we are.

Unprogrammed

For years, tight work scheduling had been my daily routine. I lived by planning, scheduling, executing. So retirement meant moving to a different regimen—short-term plans, learning that God planned my life in day-length spans. It was God's prerogative to make His plan known when the time arrived and not before. Was not His promise "As your days, so shall your strength be" (Deut. 33:25)? And doesn't this translate to "As your days, so shall your *guidance* be"? Could I—would I—accept that new mode for myself?

Admittedly, this challenge could not be assimilated all at once. Too often it remained a matter of trying to do the impossible on my own. To lessen the impact of current uncertainty, I looked back to a more reassuring past, as it were feeding upon yesterday's manna, trying to restore some semblance of "how it had always been." I didn't really face up to the more realistic questions, such as "Is it possible or wise to try to reclaim yesterday's patterns and goals? Should I expect to repeat previously successful ministries, even if on a lesser scale? Should I expect to have, as always before, a structured, programmed daily routine?" The answer was an emphatic *No!*

My problem was the inability to look back and then to let go. Looking back has potentially positive or negative outcomes. As for properly hanging on to something of the past, I could see that there was indeed a need to turn for strength and stability to the one great resource I'd established many years before—God's Word. To "hang on" to that unchanging resource was necessary and vital.

It's quite another thing, however, to hang on to something that can only impede a person's taking up new challenges to move on with God. My failure was in trying to live out "what was then," rather than "what is now." It was failure to initiate the discipline of consistently leaving behind what was no longer relevant to the present. To my shame, I was not even attempting to practice such discipline.

Please understand that my problem of looking back did not come as a consequence of the crisis I found myself in. In more subtle ways it had begun some time before, only later to become acute, even continuing on through a brief aftermath. And as might be expected, this tendency to turn back was obvious to Ruth when it was obscured to me.

The aftermath following the crisis period was the continuance of a somewhat unresolved state. Instead of moving ahead I was trying to reach back, attempting to recover the life-patterns left behind, propelled by a strange need for a phantom that no longer existed except in reminiscence. It was the attempt to reconstruct a composite of former times and places filled with friends, colleagues, events, and occupations no longer within the scope of present time. Looking back, this "crippled coping" was the very essence of futility—an illusion created in part by memory, in part by nostalgia, fantasy, and wishful thinking.

In my early or middle adult years I didn't have any tendency toward protracted nostalgia, of wanting to be somewhere else in an idealized (and of course, happier) place. Neither did anyone, certainly not Ruth, allege that I ever actually attempted to relive that past. I had seen others try. But for me there was no such attempt—*until now*.

Like most professional men, my years in the pastorate, and later in teaching, found me preoccupied with current concerns that seemed more than I could handle. In those years I only looked ahead. From the vantage point of a developing career, the future looked bright. Sure, there were occasions for recounting some past happy and significant events, momentary flashbacks. There were fantasized "if onlys" that had to do with possible opportunities missed, but nothing beyond that. Rather, the temptation lay entirely in trying to peer into the future where professional dreams seemed to lead, hoping for something grander and "more worthy of my talents."

Surely we agree that savoring cherished times is neither outside the norms of healthy reminiscence nor harmful in any way, provided such reminiscence keeps step with present reality.

Who Are We, and Where Are We Going?

Timothy K. Jones, writing in *Christianity Today* speaks of our need for a continuous inner life-narrative—knowing where we've been in order to know who we are and where we're going. He affirms, "We need not lose sight of the twists, turns, and detours that have brought us to the present."[1] Then he follows with a quote from Frederick Buechner's own self-analysis: "My interest in the past is not, I think, primarily nostalgic. Like everybody else, I rejoice in much of it and marvel at those moments when, less by effort than by grace, it comes to life again with extraordinary power and immediacy. But what quickens my pulse now is the stretch ahead rather than the one behind, and it is mainly for some clue to where I am going that I search through where I have been, for some hint as to who I am becoming or failing to become that I delve into what used to be."[2]

When I emerged from my delayed postretirement disorientation crisis, this was precisely the lesson I needed to learn. It seems true that generally we recognize that nothing of our former experience, however valued, can fill a present void. Life is not repeatable—something we know with our heads but not always with our emotions. To let previous relationships, hurts, guilts—anything once lived and left behind—become an obsessive preoccupation is futile and defeating! And quite frankly, it is denial.

Typically enough, in my own earlier adult years, the leisure necessary for nostalgia simply didn't exist. Like most younger professionals devoted to achieving their best while at the peak of their powers, current demands were all-engrossing. Full attention was needed just to give time, thought, and energy to keeping up with pressing aspects of my vocation. The sheer weight of occupational responsibilities precluded succumbing to a fixation upon what lay in the past. There was scarcely time for meeting family and social responsibilities in the present. Living the "now" was altogether pressing.

Why the Backward Look?

When I had passed the initial crisis, and Ruth and I recognized my problem was looking backward, part of recovery was to study this phenomenon as it pervades the experience of others. I dove into the relevant literature, thinking again of my years teaching sociology. That's where I could find insights.

Among the illuminating books to come into my purview was the classic work of Simone de Beauvoir, *The Coming of Age*. She asks why older people keep summoning up images of the past, and she remarks, "They are not trying to make a detailed, coherent account of their earlier years, but rather to plunge back into them. Again and again they turn over a few themes of great emotional value to themselves, and far from growing tired of this perpetual repetition, they return to it with even greater pleasure. They escape from the present; they dream of former happiness; they exorcize past misfortunes."[3]

It was not difficult to see that de Beauvoir's reflections depicted my own behavior. Here, socially speaking, was a true "postpartum syndrome." Unwittingly, I had embraced it.

Residual Problems

Even when I had regained a solid measure of health and stability, I would sometimes awaken at night with a sudden start, alarmed with the thought, "What if this should happen again? Am I still vulnerable?"

Of course, some residual effects were to be expected.

God hadn't promised I'd never again be vulnerable. The psalmist David was not delivered from *having* fears; he was delivered *from the fears he had,* fears God allowed him to have. God provides spiritual armor, but we must put it on and keep it on. And when afflictions do come, it is *His* strength, not ours, that overcomes.

These infrequent and fleeting recurrences of fear soon became fewer and farther apart until one day they were absent altogether. The burden had lifted. The enemy had been held at bay. No reason remained to fear his attacks. There was the assurance that since he had indeed been defeated at the Cross, I was on the victory side and needed only to claim that victory as my own.

Seizing Victory from Defeat

Newly strengthened by God's Spirit, I was beginning to enter into this victory the Lord had once-for-all won against the principalities and powers. It is a victory He holds out to all His own. And while persuaded victory was God's intention for me, it was also apparent that this would come only after the darkness had been endured for a season. There was a divine purpose in the darkness too! This is a truth we usually cannot grasp at the time. But after the battle's past, His purpose dawns with deep and abiding understanding.

So, in retrospect, what personal assessment can be made? All things considered, and from the perspective of God's gracious dealing with me in a unique circumstance of need, it can be said that those dark days were worth it all. An illustration from Lloyd Ogilvie provides a true though humorous clue.

Lloyd tells of learning a spiritual truth from his golf caddy, Jimmy. When Lloyd would make a poor shot that nevertheless rolled somewhere close to where he could wish, Jimmy would say, "That's a TBU shot." When Lloyd inquired, Jimmy replied, "Terrible but useful!"[4]

This wracking, depressive incident in my life—an experience repeated all-too-frequently in the lives of other retired professional and business persons particularly—was *terrible* to experience at the time, but *useful* in the hands of One who knew that spiritual advance was designed to be the ultimate outcome. The good was in the outcome (as Rom. 8:28 insists).

Let this prayer be ours:

When much is obscure to me, let me be all the more faithful to the little I can clearly see; when the distant scene is clouded, let me rejoice that at least the next step is plain.

—John Baillie[5]

3

Overcoming Losses

In her book *Necessary Losses*, Judith Viorst provides an excellent summary of one of the major retirement problems:

"Work shores up our identity; it anchors both the private and social self; it defines that self to itself and to the world. And lacking a work-place to go to, a circle of colleagues to connect with, a task to confirm our competence, a salary that puts a value on that competence, a job description that serves as a shorthand way of telling strangers who we are, we may—when we have retired—start to ask, with growing anxiety, 'Who am I?'"[1]

Viorst's words perfectly describe the combination of conditions behind my own coming to the place of asking, "Who am I?" But Viorst gets to the crux of the more generalized condition. There is no question that for many men and women retirement can best be generalized as *loss— many kinds of loss.* Whatever gains may eventually arise, the transition is initially marked by a combination of losses—loss of position, status, work roles, social network, and more. An expected result is grieving over these irretrievable losses.

Like many other major changes, loss can add up to a more generalized loss of control over one's life. And to the degree control has been a strong value attached to self-identity, sensing a loss of control is bound to be severe. On the personal level, this combination of losses involves loss of valued colleagues, possibly of associations reaching far beyond the workplace itself. Add team projects, daily routines that involve others, deadlines shared, even the office itself where you feel comfortable amid familiar surroundings. We unthinkingly take for granted the very physical surroundings we live with daily—opening the same door in the morning, locking it late afternoon. Even, the rest room down the hallway! These comprise more than routines; they are rituals. The humor that arises in the office or the despairing family problem shared by a coworker are all deeply forged bonds now severed.

Losing, Leaving, Letting Go

With any major loss we feel personally diminished and never quite the same person we were. With each loss, we acknowledge—at least in our minds—that some things are not retrievable. But the rest of our being goes on trying to deny the fact. As Viorst continues:

"We live by losing and leaving and letting go. And sooner or later, with more or less pain, we all must come to know that loss is indeed a lifelong human condition."[2]

Viorst sums it up:

"Losing is the price we pay for living. It is also the source of much of our growth and gain. Making our way from birth to death, we also have to make our way through the pain of giving up and giving up and giving up. . . . And in confronting the many losses that are brought by time and death, we become a mourning and adapting self, finding at every stage—until we draw our final breath—opportunities for creative transformations."[3]

This says it all. Now add up the important elements:

1. Losses are an inevitable part of all living.
2. The pain of loss cannot be avoided or denied.

3. Anger and resentment must be relinquished as quickly as possible or it becomes harmful.
4. Loss must be dealt with forthrightly if we are to survive and move ahead positively.
5. Grieving over major losses must be given time.
6. The challenge is to creatively turn negatives into positives.

Seeing these factors as truth, we can then acknowledge that since life is a continual adapting to loss, each of us needs to become an "adapting self." Though we cannot know what losses we may suffer, we know there will be losses.

As Viorst depicts it, this "adapting self" first becomes "a grieving self" if there are to be positive strategies for coping. So the first step to adapting incorporates grieving.

Contrary to common assumptions, grieving is not an altogether negative experience any more than loss itself is necessarily negative. When grieving is completed it moves us beyond negatives to positive loss-resolution that opens us to purposeful living once again. When the grieving process is completed it brings change to both fundamental attitudes and sense of direction, integrating the emotional and the practical in a new and positive mind-set.

As the James and Cherry *Grief Recovery Handbook* has it:

"Simply put, grief is a normal and natural response to loss. . . . We grieve for the loss of all relationships that could be held as significant and therefore emotional."[4]

In other words, loss of anything having major importance and hence a cause for grieving—whether a person, relationship, or an attachment—will bring emotional distress and a sense of personal diminution. The grieving process must run its course unimpeded. There is no value in attempting to shorten it. Worse still is to deny the grief.

There is another side to grieving. If loss is to be a means toward substantial gains, grieving—if it causes an inability to eventually move on—becomes pathological. With prolonged grieving, with inability to let go, it is possible to grieve straight into psychological illness. For the present, all future hopes have come to a dead end.

The observation of these grief recovery experts is sound:

"Since almost everything we've learned is about what we can acquire in order to feel complete or whole, the process of losing something feels wrong, unnatural, or broken."[5]

Is it any wonder, they ask, that losses so commonly prompt little more than negative responses? We look back, wishing things could be *different—or better—or repeatable*. We feel deprived of something we think might bring success, happiness, or wholeness. Unnecessarily we pile nonessential baggage onto our grieving selves, succeeding only in preventing what might very well be positive results. This, too, negates God's best for our present welfare.

The Grieving Process

From the first writing of Elisabeth Kubler-Ross, health-care experts have assumed that there are certain specific steps in the grieving process, that grieving always follows the same pattern. The bereaved person experiences shock, numbness, distress, depression, anger, denial, blaming, and so forth. There has been an established assumption that a patterned progression of grief steps is necessary, proceeding from inability to perceive and cope realistically to an eventual acceptance and adaptation, at which point ability to function resumes once again. Ability to function well doesn't come about until these steps are completed in an expected order.

But is this always the case? Is each of these steps necessary? Do they always follow in a certain order? Today this is widely questioned.

Camille Wortman of the University of Michigan and her coauthor, Roxanne Silver, have studied what they call "the myths of coping with loss." People don't always conform to a fixed pattern. They find the result of such thinking unfortunate. For example, if someone doesn't grieve openly (and considerably), the "experts" categorize this as "denial." Or if the period of grieving is too prolonged, this is categorized as "morbid self-indulgence." Judgments like these can be, and often are, seriously in error and harmful to the one who grieves.

It is more realistic to see grieving as an individual process. There are no definitions for "normal" grieving, or, as they say, "working through." Too little is known about the full spectrum of grieving to claim that a single pattern fits all persons. For one thing, your experience of losses, and coping in previous situations are preparation for the response you will make and the emotional intensity and depth that will accompany a current major loss. There are other factors having to do with what ultimate form grieving and recovery will take. As to the nature of the loss itself, there are a number of important factors—how it's interpreted, the maturity and personal resources brought to it by the person suffering the loss, the strength of support systems, and other factors. In reality, each of us has our own pattern of grieving along with an individual route to recovery.

For Christian men and women all this is a somewhat different matter considering the ways in which God enables us to meet every kind of experience of loss together with how He intends that they benefit from the grief and recovery process. He has no set pattern, rather He individualizes the recovery plan, bringing His loving care to bear uniquely on each child of His. This is His creative love for each one. God doesn't minister according to set patterns but according to individual needs and His own divine creativity.

A Time to Let Go

As severe as grieving invariably proves to be, we can be assured of this: normally there is an end. Viorst observes:

"A time will have to come when we become willing to let go of the lost relationship be it our career position in the world, a cherished person through death or divorce, a circle of close friends, or whatever. Our mourning is pathological when we cannot, or we will not, let it go."[6]

The pain of loss generally extends throughout a broad range of experiences, including retirement. Abstractly, this has to do with loss of self-definition, including images we've held of ourselves—physical appearance, attractiveness to others, statuses we've assigned ourselves, and statuses assigned us by others. Quite subconsciously, what was always important to us is how, where, and with whom we projected our best self-image. The "presentation of self," to use sociologist Irving Goffman's term, is everything—it was in times past and is now.

It is not inconsequential that we speak of "midlife crisis." Here as never before we're conscious of great transitional changes. Essentially, this is loss of "our younger self"—the only self we counted on not to change! So midlife changes sound a warning in terms of the future. For one thing, physical changes in the 40s are unmistakable and irreversible. As a pastor friend in his late 30s said to me: "I recognize that I'm no longer able to play a game of softball one day and walk the next!" Another observes, "I've exchanged weight *lifting* for weight *watching!*" How many of us—with a nervous smile—ruefully acknowledge this!

Not Any Easier

All too plainly, the image in the mirror tells the story: "I'm no longer the same person as before." Or "I don't have what I once had." Try as we may, whatever clever end-runs seem promising, each coming year brings added physical and emotional costs. In disbelief we ask, "Why is it so much harder to come up with the physical and emotional payment? Why the decreasing attractiveness of the social amenities of my position?" Simply put, despite fitness programs—or whatever else—we are *tired of it all!* There is a wistfulness over life losing its zest.

Midlife sounded the message strong and clear: with passing time, life doesn't get easier. *But, wait, were we listening then? Did we take it seriously then? How does this process affect us in the retirement transition?*

For a moment, trace the course from a different angle. In our 40s and 50s, relationships with our children underwent critical changes as did relationships with our parents. The children were moving off into a separate universe while we become parents to our parents. Some families are faced with devoting more time caring for aging parents than the time devoted to raising their own children. In contrast, many single mothers today are leaning on their retired parents to raise their children while they themselves are working to support the family.

Inevitably as a retiree your relationship with your spouse undergoes changes in anticipation of newly emerging roles. The empty nest—most destabilizing to a wife and her mothering role—is something a husband cannot avoid sharing. As a retired husband and wife, you are not just retirees, but a couple again, your life focused on the primary relationship you share and on your social needs as a couple. It may have been a long time since this type of closeness placed demands upon you. Equally serious, the health of your marriage may be in question.

Each change-point—young adulthood to midlife, midlife to retirement—represents major detachments. As Dr. George Pollock observes, "One might describe this process as mourning for former states of the self, as if these states represented lost objects."[7] Daniel Levinson says that often we feel suspended between past and future, struggling to overcome the gap that separates them. In *A Grief Observed*, C. S. Lewis used the same expression:

"I think I am beginning to understand why grief feels like suspense. It comes from the frustration of so many impulses that had become habitual. . . . Now their target is gone. I keep on, through habit, fitting an arrow to the string; then I remember and I have to lay the bow down."[8]

That Disconnected Feeling

Upon reaching retirement we suddenly are detached from even the recent past. Our strongest feeling is that of disconnection. We recognize how fragile are the threads of connection, more than we thought.

Part of the crisis, of course, is aging. Shocking is the realization that aging no longer refers only to our parents, but to us! We need to laugh at some of what is occurring. Too much of life is frustration and distress.

As you begin to notice the aging process, you become aware that the compulsive drive that marked earlier vocational development has begun to lessen. Ambition notably recedes and achievement goals slip from your expectations. Then comes the realization that not everything was worth the effort previously assigned to it. The very nature of reward itself underwent change. Work-values lose both clarity and drive.

With the cluster of losses suffered by midlife, you'd think we'd be prepared for those that come with retirement. But it doesn't seem to work that way, at least not for everyone.

The pain of loss, indigenous to retirement, extends through the range of experiences in every transition adults pass through. Each transition commonly follows one similar pattern—leaving, losing, and letting go.

When we grieve the death of a spouse, we grieve for more than the spouse alone. We grieve the loss of an intimate friend, perhaps provider and/or protector, partner in parenthood, companion in social interaction, spiritual encourager, and more. We grieve over being no longer part of a pair—the loss of couple-identity. Translate this to losses at retirement and it's easy to see the connection. A whole way of life is altered so that there, too, the grieving process is in order.

The greater any loss is interpreted to be, the more traumatic the aftershocks. The positive side, says Viorst, is this: "Through mourning we come to accept the difficult changes that loss must bring—and then we begin to come to the end of mourning."[9] For most people recovery comes about in a reasonable amount of time. Of course, for some it is more complete and more positively accomplished than for others.

Claiming Control over Oneself

As James and Cherry point out, recovery consists in claiming control over one's circumstances instead of letting circumstances claim control over us. Complete recovery is determined by a variety of conditions, most of them resident within an individual's own personality, not in external circumstances. For instance, recovery is near completion when once again memories can be enjoyed and reminiscences no longer precipitate unbearably painful feelings of deprivation and when there no longer remains a compulsion to cling unrealistically to the past.

A good recovery allows you to freely acknowledge that it's perfectly OK to look back, to think negatively about losses—even once in awhile to feel less than fully recovered. Reality never need be denied or repressed. It's all part of normal experience and in no way signals a major setback. The first step in recovery is acceptance of the normality of the experience.

James and Cherry locate the final ascent to recovery at the point where the individual's ability to talk about their loss and adjustment helps others get through theirs. Sharing is a vital part of recovery, a positive consequence of suffering loss when compensating features take the upper hand. Retirees need support of others with whom they can share their experience and in the process sense the commonality of what is transpiring in both of their lives.

I can vouch for this. My own path to full recovery was lighted with bright new assurances when I found myself sharing the experience with retired friends, many of whom were pastors. Sharing itself is a form of therapy. For me, sharing became a perfectly comfortable thing to do. Through sharing insights and aims, these very articulations were consolidated and strengthened in my own thinking.

Along the way I found retirees who would hear me discuss the dynamics of the retirement crisis yet were unwilling to disclose their own fears and struggles. Things changed as the subject was discussed in terms of my own experience. Then, typically, there would come a flood of questions that expressed their own struggles. That concern, you can be sure, is out there; I merely tapped into it. A recent seminar I conducted on these subjects confirmed how great the need and how frequent the crisis. This, I'm convinced, is indeed the hidden agenda of a considerable number of retirees.

Attachment and Loss

In 1980, John Bowlby, British psychiatrist and child development authority, published three volumes titled *Attachment and Loss.* There he reported the active role of loss in relation to depression. He cited, among others, the studies of G. W. Brown, T. Harris, and J. R. Copeland who claim that loss and disappointment are central features of most events, bringing about clinical depression. While for the most part it might be a death, or a child leaving home for a distant place, or marital breakdown, still some 20 percent said it was the loss of a job or the move to retirement.[10]

Another investigator, Eugene Paykel, found that two-thirds of the events preceding the onset of depressive illness could be classified as losses. As a retiree you should understand the mechanisms of this process to cope with the continued losses sure to mark your path.

This connection has caught the attention of contemporary Christian psychologists. Archibald Hart, director of Clinical Training at the Graduate School of Psychology at Fuller Theological Seminary, in a chapter titled "Depression as a Response to Loss," writes "I believe that the key to understanding nearly all of the reactive depressions is to see them as a response to a sense of loss."[11]

Therapy for Transient Depressions

Hart distinguishes reactive depression from neurotic depression. His concern is not with the pervasive state of depression rooting in deep-seated anxiety or alienation, nor with clinical depression. Reactive depression is not treated by medication but generally by therapeutic counseling that seeks to understand the social conditions that brought about the depressive reaction. If possible, these social conditions must be changed. At the very least they should be accepted, while coping measures are put into place. This is the whole field we call social psychology. And the retiree is relieved from thinking the next step is to a psychiatrist's office.

Intangible Losses

Our prime concern is with what is called "abstract loss," the loss of intangibles. There are *tangible losses*—loss of a spouse, job, office associates, children who leave home. These are object-losses, and there is no mystery about these. Coping can be straightforwardly dealt with. Quite different are *intangible losses*—love, hope, status— subjective in nature, losses experienced *in the abstract,* the less-easily recognized and often not understood. With these we are unable to pinpoint a loss-object. Not that intangible losses are less real, simply more difficult to understand and deal with. They can be extremely acute and distressing, and generally require therapeutic counseling.

For example, look at hope. Loss of hope can result from inability to perceive a future for yourself. The future appears shut off. In these instances, people lose hope in themselves, in other people, in the events they're caught up in. Even hope in God's providential care may become shaken. For most Christians this usually is a transient occurrence. Hope returns as God brings His sustaining grace to bear. Nonetheless, the process may call for extensive counseling assistance.

Retirement is a particularly relevant scenario. When you no longer see yourself as prominent in the public eye, when you feel isolated, removed from the working public and no longer needed, you are experiencing abstract, intangible losses. You may not be able to adequately interpret what is happening. Retirees are peculiarly subject to changes in the abstract. Hart concurs that grief is the appropriate response to loss, describing the grief process in ways similar to those we've looked at.

In connection with abstract losses, in my own experience there was a strange nagging to make up for failures accumulated along life's way. It no longer appeared possible to reengage opportunities long since gone by the boards. This recognition only exacerbated my feeling of hopelessness tinged with guilt.

Of course, we all have regrets over past failures; none of us differs in this regard. To any thoughtful older Christian, at some point or another this brings pain, the most common time being retirement. Why? For one thing, we retirees have greater time and occasion to reflect upon these unforgotten, regrettable instances. Failures of former years not only appear more luminous but also tend to be more than a little exaggerated.

How easily we're led to dwell on lost opportunities, magnifying occasions when we might have exerted some helpful effort but didn't, might have tried to meet another's needs but didn't, might have witnessed for the Lord but didn't. Now that these opportunities can no longer be pursued, there looms more significantly than ever before a sense of failure because of duties omitted. For those who otherwise have been effective job performers, conscience tends to render an accusatory accounting by dredging up the failures. But we cannot live by regrets, nor does God ask this of us. He bids us accept His forgiveness where required and then proceed to forgive ourselves in Jesus' name. Happily, past opportunities now gone do pave the way for present opportunities to take their place. These are our more legitimate concerns.

Another aspect of the feeling of failure is that reduced activity may be interpreted as indolence—opportunities consciously wasted (the picture of "God's servants faithful to the end, dying with their boots on"). Among those of us coming from a serving background, who early responded to the ministry, this call never vacates our heart of hearts. Remorse over failures to minister only exacerbates such guilt feelings.

Doubtless, the sense of failure is most frequently the curse of perfectionists. Their case will be taken up shortly, but just to start you thinking about this, many successful men and women have tended to be perfectionists. In retirement some of them try to live up to the adulation they received over their years of superior work achievement. Strangely, from a perfectionist's point of view, looking at life as it was before retirement is to see a sad chronicle of failures, large and small. Retirement then becomes "the last chance" to rectify past mistakes and failures. And so they continue in their perfectionism. It is only self-defeating. Perfectionists take note!

There is also the voice of a harassing conscience. That agonizes, "How is it possible to relax in retirement and be so self-indulgent when there's so much to make up for?" Here the voice of conscience cannot accept the realities of human imperfection. Again, it places what we do (and do not do) above who and what we are as struggling fellow travelers in an imperfect world. It is another aspect of loss and possible cause for depression.

Return with me to tangible losses and another subject we cannot disregard—such realities as the growing limitations of health and energy. There will come the time when the capacity to grasp opportunities "out there" is critically diminished. We need to settle it once and for all that personal limitations are likely to increase from now on. But then we can turn to quiet witnessing, to a life devoted to loving God and His people, perhaps just serving in little but significant and caring ways.

There is a nearly universal sense of loss that accompanies the knowledge of having lived at less than our absolute best—not as failures, but simply less than one's best. Though true of every life and generally a matter of oversensitivity, this regret must be dealt with like any other loss. Eventually, time brings acceptance of the less-than-best past with whatever failures and lost opportunities occasioned pain and regret. In time we stop struggling with it.

Abundant Grace

For Christians, acceptance of an imperfect past needs to be committed to God's forgiving grace. As forgiven persons, we also need to forgive ourselves and live in the reality of forgiveness. When we do, we're relieved of compulsive striving to make up what cannot be made up. What we can be assured of is that there are new opportunities to be grasped, spiritual ministries now within our capabilities. We can commit ourselves once more to attempting our best, not that such efforts make up for past failures but to provide the joy and privilege of present ministering.

When it all boils down, most important to our personal progress is understanding that it is not any one or more losses themselves but *our interpretation of losses* that brings depression. This is why different people react differently to the same kinds of losses.

In retrospect I see my own depressive experience as serving a healthy function, not that I could have predicted this result at the time. Gripping, agonizing depression with its confused and hopeless introspection was all part of the shock of loss. Mourning that loss was enduring a process that otherwise I strenuously would have avoided. It brought to my attention just how deeply I interpreted the loss of status, roles, and associations, and how severe were the costs in subconscious pain. It was hard reality, but it was healthful to recognize it and take its measure.

Retirement is freighted with dreams of an ideal life of freedom to do many new things. However, invariably we hear of retirement's lost dreams and the difficulty of accepting and coping with the loss. For example, one couple dreams of having a summer cottage or recreational vehicle. Now retired, they say to themselves, "This is going to be *real* living!" But the hard reality of insufficient assets prevents the dream becoming reality or from long continuing to be so. They can't afford the upkeep.

Another couple has exciting dreams of travel never before possible, but decreasing health doesn't permit it. Travel is physically not worth the effort.

Still another couple dreams of being free to relocate near their children. But the children do not seem keen for the idea, and friends advise against it. Plans come to a halt, and dreams turn to disillusionment. They decide not to move anywhere.

Then there are dreams cut short by death of a spouse. Dreams turn to nightmares. Joy is displaced by grief and hopes dissipate. Every possibility seems to mock the grieving individual who has lost a mate.

So, whether it's money, circumstances, health, death— every loss has its way of turning dreams to ashes. The loss side of life's ledger lengthens together with the limitations of the aging process.

Of course, the story does not always end with sadness. There are gains of another nature to be explored. So, in light of these things, remember: losses themselves can't make losers!

For sturdy hearts dependent upon God, losses only make room for the special gains that God has planned. He is not unaware of our needs. Losses can become the soil in which God's people flower! The first condition is full trust in His providential care. Surrender to Christ always means, as martyred missionary Jim Elliot said so eloquently and prophetically before his own life was given in its prime, that we sometimes must give what we cannot keep in order to gain what we cannot lose. Committed Christians are true winners, not losers!

So we grieve over losses—whatever they may be—then relinquish the past for the present, looking with hope to the future, knowing that is where God is. We take the way of faith, trusting Him to guide, learning more fully the deepest secret of these bonus years!

4

Letting Go and Moving On

Why are we drawn so compulsively toward trying to re-capture a life now gone? What is so seductive about past years other than fond reminiscences? It is one thing to catch ourselves looking back at the past, but now the more serious question is why we try to actually go back, if only in our minds. Why is this compulsion so dangerous to successful retirement adjustment? How do we distinguish the *helpful* from the *hurtful* in our attachments to the past?

First, the past is all we know for certain; it's already ours by experience; it is the one vast intangible we *possess*. A vacuum is filled in so far as a newly retired man or woman stands peering into a largely unforeseeable future and hence is a bit frightened. The present is still tentative while the future is altogether unknown. For this reason alone the past is much more comfortable to contemplate. So we find security as well as the evidence of our cherished self-identification in clinging to a past that cannot change.

The Role Nostalgia Plays

Second, we tend to be captives to nostalgia with reference to what we've loved, lost, and left behind—familiar neighborhoods, close friends, significant career, meaningful social circles, fulfilling activities, important statuses, and the multiple roles we've played. In other words, it is about all the people, events, and involvements of a lifetime. This aura of nostalgic reminiscence is given great force by our emotional attachments to that memoried past.

We need to be aware that nostalgic reminiscence is selective, retaining memories we never want to lose.

But *reminiscence-plus-nostalgia* can, and often does, exacerbate the problems of a smooth retirement transition. Reminiscence is spontaneous recall, useful for illuminating the overall inventory of our personal history. One prominent psychiatrist explains: "By monitoring the process of change that inevitably occurs over time, reminiscence contributes in a fundamental way to the stability and integrity of the personality."[1]

Reminiscence provides continuity to the historical awareness of our life. Originally the word nostalgia meant "homesickness"—a painful longing for joys attached to people and places now removed. The word comes from the Greek "to return home" and rather curiously carried the implication of a painful condition. In the evolving etymology, the word came to mean that which a person longs for, that which belongs to another time—usually past time. This accurately defines our problem.

Nostalgia can be terribly regressive in that it shuns the present and the future to feed on the past. So nostalgia may be either normal or pathological, depending on whether or not it is compulsive and obsessive. The retiree who lives unrealistically in nostalgia is leaning toward pathological nostalgia. Unfortunately, the person so compelled is generally the last to recognize it, and so is not in position to deal with it.

The problem with nostalgia is the way it distorts and blows things out of proportion, frequently incorporating exaggerated emotions that further complicate the overblown picture.

Many retirees struggle against compulsive nostalgia over that which has been lost or left behind. Not that this is unnatural, but it can pose an obstacle to making adjustments to the new life of retired living. Recognizing this is the first step in dealing with it.

Peter Kreeft adds a somber note about what causes the aging person to indulge nostalgic reminiscence. It's not the desire to relive the past but rather not wanting to look forward to the time of likely disablement and death. The non-Christian may well wonder whether death will forever end the ability to remember the nostalgic past that is so meaningful, forever banishing those happy memories. In Kreeft's words,

"The experience of longing for the past that is unattainably gone is our deep nostalgia brought about by the knowledge of death. It is seeing our past with the eyes of death before we die."[2]

We *Are* Our Social History

What we need to remember is that reminiscence is one of the greatest features of human existence. Each of us is a product of past experiences. What we are now is the accumulation of all that we have ever been. To know ourselves as unique individuals different from all others, having our own self-definition, seeing ourselves in a sweeping panorama of individual social history. We cannot detach ourselves from that history. *We are our social history; our social history is us!*

Inescapably, people and events filed away in memory form the content of our personal history, the record of how we've come to be the persons we are. Seen together, the continuity of past and present validates who we are in the here and now. To relive these memories is to keep alive all the elements that contributed toward making us what we've become. And because what we're continuing to become extends into the future—of which we know nothing for certain—our "becoming" attaches most significantly to that which brought us to our own particular present.

So we grant that the past is concretely deposited in our personalities and memory, remaining there throughout our lifetime. Apart from amnesia, senility, or Alzheimer's, it cannot be dislodged. In this history, this extended narrative indelibly written and open to reminiscence, we see our true selves in the lengthened shadow of the countless changes making up that history. At any given moment, the meaning of our life is the sum of all the meanings we've processed up to that point.

Jules Willing summarizes the problem as we face it at retirement:

> We have spent all our working lives creating our own personal history, our eyes fixed on the future consequences of our acts and decisions. There has always been a next stage in our careers, the events of which we are formulating in the present. . . . But now for the first time we have reached the place where our story stops; there is no next stage. . . . For the first time, we can measure the entire distance from where we started a life-time ago to the farthest place we have reached.[3]

Of course, for the Christian there is a "next stage," not merely an earthly end-point. The better part of memory is extending the best of our becoming into what we look forward to being in heaven. So our self-identity is continually formed through the whole of life, and the truly memorable aspects are the spiritual steps and growth it represents. Retirement must be fitted into the best of this process.

Timothy Jones quotes from Frederick Buechner's own self-analysis:

> My interest in the past is not, I think, primarily nostalgic. Like everybody else, I rejoice in much of it and

marvel at those moments when, less by effort than by grace, it comes to life again with extraordinary power and immediacy . . . But what quickens my pulse now is the stretch ahead rather than the one behind, and it is mainly for some clue to where I am going that I search through where I have been, for some hint as to who I am becoming or failing to become that I delve into what used to be.[4]

Saul Bellow in *Mr. Sammler's Planet* stated, "Everybody needs his memories. They keep the wolf of insignificance from the door."

Memory Modifying Itself to Suit Desire

Reminiscing is never truly objective, and nostalgic reminiscence always less so, partly because both comprise an exercise in subjective reflection. Our past is modified as memory creatively rewrites it. For memory, you see, is both selective and creative, having a genius for transforming the actual past into an idealized, more desirable past. As someone said, "Here we pass from autobiography to novel." Mentally, we reconstruct the past in its best lights. Thus good old days, fantastic places, and momentous events are all richly colored by memory's creative genius. Selectively, we remember most vividly what we wish, or need, to remember, and for the most part that was the good and the pleasant. Mentally we toss out what we wish to forget.

Reminiscence, insofar as memory crafts a new past out of the old, amending it to make it appear better than it was, quite naturally we have no reason to protest such advantageous reconstruction. So we tend to do nothing about that. We then rehearse it over and over, each new telling of the story sounding more authentic than the one before! In no time at all we have a past marvelously transmuted into a version worth reciting! Always it is the good old days, the team that never lost, the great job only "I" could handle. We especially find pleasure remembering the idealized past at times when present experiences seem to have diminishing importance. That's the hidden danger.

Discipline of Relinquishment

"Aging," someone remarked, "is when we experience fewer and fewer things for the first time and more and more things for the last time." As another suggested, "Aging is when the sum total of our memories exceeds the sum total of our hopes." So we are called to the discipline of not letting the past crowd our minds to the point that we dismiss the present and future.

Common to Us All

We've all regressed into wishful thinking about a supposedly uncomplicated youth or perhaps some previous period now idealized as "the best time of my life." For the retiree this can center upon the years of vocational challenges, hard work, and reward—time totally invested in a career now still seen in the rosy light of reminiscence and its nostalgic component. Looking back is so often a coping mechanism, an escapist diversion, a promising deliverance from unmanageable circumstances. Dwelling on some former period in our personal history can make the past a defense against the forbidding present and the unknowable future for which that past was exchanged.

Of course, memories are by no means limited to fond ones. We carry negative memories into retirement as unneeded baggage—deep hurts, unremitting guilts, unrequited loves, foolish or deliberate misdeeds. Our minds are shackled to painful, alienated relationships to people whose forgiveness we need, or who need our forgiveness. Often it's this kind of unfinished business that draws our minds back, driving us again and again to rethink the course we've taken, as though thinking about it can correct it.

There is a far more positive question: "What might we seek out so as to restore, repair, or release something needful from the past?" With God's gift of these bonus years of retirement, what we have done or left undone is not as important as what we still might do. What is hard for us to grasp is that however cruel life's negative situations have been, however dark the deeds we've done—or had done to us—the only continuing claim those remembrances can make upon us is *what we permit* them to have. It is our choice. Of course, if confessing some wrong to an offended party is still possible, if forgiveness is expressed—even restitution made wherever possible—then memory is a beneficial action-prompter. But much of the negative past can only be placed under the forgiveness of God. Generally, it is no longer possible to recreate the conditions of the past that would enable our actually dealing with it as we might wish.

Whenever some dark specter out of the past gives birth to a bitter, unforgiving spirit, the sure antidote for release and cleansing is prayer. But once done, to continue bringing these matters to God again and again is to misuse reminiscence and to deny the forgiveness God has already put in place. He wants us to put out of mind all that He's forgiven and forgotten. Too often the problem is refusal to forgive ourselves. Furthermore, to bring it up is a failure to lay hold of the victory we possess in Christ, victory that needs only to be appropriated by faith and acted out. We are to possess our possessions in Christ; one of which is a forgiving spirit learned at the feet of the One who forgives us (Eph. 4:32).

Enemy of the Present

So often a present association triggers the "reminiscence-plus-nostalgia" event. Before we know it, we have a vivid reminder of something mentally long-repressed—a person, group, place, or series of events. For a brief moment, and with no apparent reason, some little scene from the past shines brightly and rivets our attention. Momentarily it is a fixation, something so powerful, so compelling, as to disable us from embracing the present with its demands, opportunities, and responsibilities. It has power to effectively immobilize us. We need disciplined, conscious attention to bring its quick elimination.

Helpful Strategies

There are specific things that can be done.

1. *Discipline yourself to concentrate on "the now."* With firm deliberation put aside the *"then"* whenever you sense it dominating your thoughts and emotions. If this sounds simple or easy, it never is until the habit has become second nature! So stick with it!

2. *Recognize that memories of a blissful, secure past are part exaggeration and part illusion.* The nostalgic connection is apparent: When our daily routines are slowed to meet the lessened pace of retirement we are most easily seduced into turning our vision backward. When we experience new insecurities, we're tempted to think the greater security lies "back there somewhere." Deliberately concede that some realities of your life-history are forever gone. Give them a kind burial!

Lewis Carroll, author of *Alice in Wonderland,* has a great insight for us. "It's a poor sort of memory that only works backwards." Inasmuch as memory serves to remind us of future possibilities we've stored there, let those memories *work forward* as well! This is where God is prepared to meet you. *He* isn't looking backward!

Don't Put Life on Hold

Can retirees afford to put life on hold? Is this God's plan? If the first step is letting go and moving on, what is the next step? Do we have the option of putting life on hold? If retirement is to be something more, what exactly is it? Some people think of retirement as the time when they "kick back and really start living." With little thought, they add, "Isn't that what retirement's all about?" Then comes the shock of arriving at retirement and asking all-too-soon, "What's ahead for me now? Surely, there's more? How can I live a truly meaningfully life now?" For sure, it isn't putting life on hold! Retirees cannot move on without putting in place a solid purpose and plan.

Life, if only temporarily on hold, quickly becomes stagnant. Lack of direction strikes at the very psychological heart of retirement. We need a vision of future possibilities along with a firm commitment to fulfill God's will as He unfolds it. The very last thing a thoughtful retiree should settle for is to put life on hold. It has been said, "You can't avoid a *wrong* direction by going *no* direction!"

As for approaching retirement with expectations, be aware of having overexpectations, false expectations, shifting expectations, or no expectations. For a variety of reasons, things may not turn out to be what you thought—often less, sometimes far less. Happily, it may be far more! It goes back to adequate forethought and thinking and planning ahead to reduce the chances of wrong expectations.

"Worth" Ethic

In his book *Retirement Without Fear*, Lee Butcher touches on the distinction between work and worth.[5] He cites a University of Michigan study of America's work ethic. Along with a work ethic, he suggests, is the need for a comparable "worth ethic." What this involves, fundamentally, is removing the concept of "worth" from "work." Does it seem a radical notion to focus on *the worth of persons apart from the worth of their work?* Not at all.

For Christians, the "worth ethic" gets at the very heart of work as part of the stewardship of time and talent—the concept of life as a worthy use of God's endowments. Still, the overall message of Scripture is that true worth derives from *who we are* much more than from *what we do.* Both, of course, have their place, but the ultimate value resides in the person, not in the work. Work-worth is a passing, ever-changing phenomenon, whereas worth of persons is an unchanging eternal reality.

Let me illustrate from my own career as pastor, professor, counselor, and writer—all occupations that satisfied my sense of self-identity. As a retiree, most of these work roles were either gone or diminished to the point of no longer defining me as a person. I needed to realize that I was someone special to God apart from whatever I chose to do and however anyone else might regard me. The quality of my life before His eyes was most important. This realization became critical sometime after retirement's relatively good but less-than-well-thought-out start. Along the way I was seeing myself as a changing person, some of which I liked, some I didn't like, and some of which caused deep concern and pain. I'd thought of retirement as living my life for Ruth and me. It wasn't working. I wasn't investing my life wisely. I should have known this, perhaps did, but didn't want to come to terms with it.

Here is a distinction we Christian retirees need to understand well. We are to exchange *"worth as employed worker under obligation"* for *"worth as child of God whether working or not."* This alters our whole perspective. Each of us needs to see beyond self-achievement in order to see God's design for who and what He wants us to be. In the end, our worth equates with what He values—what we are *to Him.* And as life grows shorter, this becomes more important. Primarily, worth resides within ourselves, as persons who belong to Him. This recognition is stimulus for the cultivation of self-worth through proper use of our retirement years—the bonus years He's given us.

One other facet deserves attention. What we *do* for God and His kingdom is not what establishes our worth to God. Relationship is first! What matters most is our continuing growth in Christ. This is the true imperative of the Christian life! We possess inherent worth as unique persons who, though fallen, are redeemed and meant to reflect God's glory. This biblical concept enables us to see our lives as meaningful in the highest sense. Created from individualized molds, so to speak, we are meant for individually-tailored ends. God never sees us as other than individuals redeemed in order to glorify Him, however each of us does so in our own different way. Even our "retirement calling" is uniquely individual in His eyes.

To remove wrong-headed views of worth based on work, we need what Paul Tournier calls "reconversion"—ability to see personal life as a developing whole, a process of maturing throughout its entire length. Reconversion enables us to respond to new interests, new activities, new relationships. In sum, reconversion equates with the emphasis upon personal growth. How well this goes with the apostle's words:

"I appeal to you therefore, brethren, by the mercies of

God, to present your bodies as a living sacrifice, holy and acceptable to God, which is your spiritual worship. Do not be conformed to this world but be transformed by the renewal of your mind, that you may prove what is good and acceptable and perfect" (Rom. 12:1-2).

5

Discovering New People and New Roles

So long as we haven't yet learned how to handle the replacement of former life patterns with new ones, it is tempting to slip into apathy and passivity. But how can we hope to discover new meanings, new interests, new objectives if our gaze is fixed only on the things of earth? This is the heart of reconversion. If we seek to be meaningfully occupied for Him, and seek to know His plan, the transition will go smoothly and usually quite quickly.

Your thinking may revert to the mentality that dominated your working years. Subconsciously we may still think "the more I *do,* the more I *am,* and the more I *produce,* the greater will be my reward." But when we recognize our worth doesn't reside in anything we can do, reclaim, repeat, or achieve in the same way as before, then the status "retiree" will develop increasing conformity to the will of Christ. Our first and deepest concern is that of loving and serving God—the God we shall soon meet—and secondly that of winning the rewards of His kingdom.

We should seriously seek to know and employ the individualized gifts of the Spirit promised in 1 Cor. 12:7, 11. Each of us have a part in the rich diversity of ministry God has appointed. Such giftedness by the Spirit will inspire far more than visions of a leisure-time world with a laid-back lifestyle characterized by countless pleasures but little growth, little meaning, little of significance.

Friendships

We retirees soon discover how diversely populated is the world of retired persons. If we've relocated, even a new church fellowship becomes part of adapting to the new environment. It too is where we do not as yet have a base of fellowship. We soon learn that none of us can expect new friendships to be a reincarnation of the old office gang or the former church bunch! To begin with, as new friendships are needed, so too is the effort needed to make them happen.

It's easy to pout: "New friends just aren't like old friends." No, of course not! Should we think otherwise? As Ruth and I found with our circle of new friends, a few are providing as close and meaningful a bond as our former longtime friends. Truth is, deep friendships can be either long-term or of recent origin. Quite naturally, we delight to see old friends who live at a distance, even if infrequently. We can count on them being the same as always, special because of our long history together, some of them going back to when we all were starting our families and raising our children. Time and distance cannot change that. But new friends satisfy ongoing week by week needs. By and large we select them because they share the same faith, lifestyle, and concerns. It is good to recall that we are new friends to them as they are to us. Cementing friendships is a two-way process.

Leisure: The New Luxury

In order to adequately think through the full meaning of retired living, we have to come to terms with the new-found luxury called leisure time. Here we bump head-on into a harsh reality. The very leisure we've looked forward to becomes a problem down the line, even a burden. It is doubtful we'd ever guessed that so radical a reorientation toward leisure would take place.

During working years, leisure consisted of brief, intermittent breaks extracted from busy work schedules. Generally, family activities were the objective with planned summer vacations or national holiday weekends when the children were out of school. These were essentially recreational episodes sandwiched into an otherwise unrelieved occupational grind. We referred to them as "breaks."

During midyears, when the nest emptied, leisure scheduling became more opportune, more flexible. We fathers and mothers were a couple again. For the first time there was a preview of what leisure might one day become, freed from obligations relating not only to work but children as well. But was this a true preview of retirement leisure?

Early on, I had to learn that quality-living in retirement meant stopping from a concentration on what had been *given up* to what is being *taken up*. Leisure challenged this perspective. Now, those short intermittent leisure occasions, breaks, have been exchanged for a long-term leisure lifestyle. Leisure jumped to the forefront, no longer an incidental element, no longer a reward for days worked, but the new status quo, the major base of retirement.

What do we do with unlimited time for ourselves? Will it be employed for trivial ends? Good yet self-centered ends? Or best of all, for worthy ends that satisfy the inner person, ends conducive to personal growth and service? What about making a significant advance in spiritual development? Then, too, does a leisured life have costs as well as rewards? If so, what do we expect to get for the price we pay?

Less Worthy or More?

The new leisure is unparalleled freedom to choose either less worthy or more worthy use of time and abilities.

Not that these are altogether either-or; there is place for both. If we are engaged in ministries, we can properly reserve room for purely leisure activities. These activities, including the recreational, are an important part of maintaining good health. All avenues for self-improvement as well as spiritual growth are to be encouraged. The challenge lies in finding the proper balance.

Not Freedom for Freedom's Sake

Freedom is not an end in itself, but a means to achieving other ends. As with the use of any gift God gives, we are responsible for the time at our disposal.

From now on, our daily patterns will be organized around this dominant leisure mode. Soon these patterns come to order our active retirement years. Remember, inasmuch as all behaviors are patterned, once these retirement patterns become habitual they are not easily altered. So "think leisure" wisely and plan carefully! It's a self-directed life you're now living!

The fundamental difference with the new leisure is twofold: *meaning* and *structure*. Leisure is no longer something sandwiched in whenever possible. Neither is it essentially recreational. The new leisure is serious business (meaning) if it is to serve worthy purposes.

We need to balance leisure with whatever occupations we choose (structure), avoiding letting leisure become "a glut"—that is, an overindulgence, a surfeit, a waste.

It remains a curious thing that we formerly used to chafe because work-years didn't provide enough leisure to suit us. Now we chafe because unlimited leisure is not sufficiently challenging or satisfying!

Does thinking about balancing leisure with work perhaps strike you as incongruous *(Aren't we retirees through with working?).* Leisure and work are equally necessary elements for successful retirement. An ideal combination is possible. It is not that work is *exchanged* for leisure; not at all. Both continue, but simply in different modes. Each is meant to contribute in its own way to our development as whole persons. Paul Tournier's comment is on target: "Work brings development in depth because of the specialization it requires. Leisure counterbalances with development in breadth because of the diversity of interests it cultivates."[1]

Reward or Responsibility?

One popular but misleading notion is that leisure is the reward for having fulfilled our work-years. We see leisure being hawked as the goal toward which working years are directed—earned reward. This is not true; leisure is simply what is dominant after working years are over.

While ours is a culture that still values work for itself as well as for material and personal rewards, today's culture elevates leisure as work's chief reward. Note how the entertainment industry is programmed to dominate major timeslots. Someone remarked insightfully that modern Americans work more leisurely and employ their leisure more seriously. The common expectation is that leisure is to be maximized. Whole industries—among the most successful in the nation—are dependent on selling this proposition to the American people. Understandably, when one's life has been devoted to working for 40 years or so, the prospect of leisure has tremendous drawing power. So the theme is constantly drummed into us: "Retire as early as possible; enjoy the best of the American dream, and make the most of it!" Although man doesn't live by leisure alone, many try. But using freedom to *be, do,* and *go,* is not the whole story. Freedom has its nobler purposes to fulfill.

In recent years there has been much reassessment of the push to an even earlier retirement age, as to its advantages and disadvantages. Yet not a few men and women find themselves *retiring from retirement*—and for thoughtful reasons. They're discovering that retirement isn't the be-all and end-all. When a person retires early and has good health, it can be assumed they will want to be reemployed in some fashion—perhaps under different conditions, but employed nonetheless. These trends have been spurred by millions of today's "baby boomers." This segment of the population represents approximately 76 million people born from World War II in 1946 and on as late as 1964. These are people who have arrived or will arrive at retirement's doorstep all too soon.

Retirement in American life is about to undergo a major change in the way Americans think and plan. A 50-year trend toward ever-earlier retirement is now in flux. Anti-work sentiments are increasingly being wrung out of the economic system for broader and more positive perspectives.

Boomers will stretch out their working lives, extending their productive years. They will move in and out of new and varied careers, not viewing retirement as a clean break, a single event, but rather as a gradual process taking a series of steps. They will enter other occupations on their own terms, sometimes choosing part-time positions for a given period of time so as to be free to engage in activities they wish to pursue at particular times and for certain lengths of time. More and more they will be world citizens. The concept now coming into play is called "Bridge Jobs." Boomers taking this road will be less likely to define who they are by what they're doing at present. They will see a less-defined line between actively working at, say, 55 and whatever they might happen to be doing the next day, or for that matter 5 years or so down the road. For one thing, boomers will be more physically fit and healthy at earlier retirement age. They will live longer, with adequate health and opportunities to be productive.

According to an April 1997 Roper Starch survey commissioned by AARP, the vast majority of boomers intend to continue working part-time, with a lesser percentage planning to work full-time. The majority say they will want to work because they like to work. A significant percent plan to go into business for themselves, many because they can quit commuting, work at home, and enjoy flexible hours with work suited to accommodate entirely new objectives. Other reasons include not wanting to be dependent on their children during retirement years, desire for greater financial security, and little or no confidence that Social Security and Medicare provisions will continue viable. This is a seismic shift from 1997 when fewer than 12 percent of persons 65 and older held jobs. And this sea change, as we say, implies the need for greater midcareer training and an altered design of how they'll acquire and manage their retirement accounts.

For retirees today these trends have interesting implications. In companies anticipating such changes, boomers are even now gearing up to put in place the creation of more opportunities for part-time employment with flexible hours for all persons, including seniors. Even now, the idea of employing seniors for home computer work as well as company-based jobs is attractive inasmuch as it takes keen minds and experienced backgrounds but not physical output and undesirable commuting. It allows for breaks around home during the day, breaks to do other things like gardening or pursuing a subject on the Internet. Time is always theirs to use as they wish. Different kinds of employment contracts will be available to suit new work conditions. These are the coming trends.

A friend of mine retired from Lockheed's engineering

team at Vandenberg Air Force Base. To fulfill a lifelong dream, he purchased a large motor home. He and his wife launched out on a five-month trip across the nation. Shortly after they returned, he quietly sold the motor home, quit talking about travel, and began looking for an occupation. He chose to help in the construction of a new Elks Club building and be a part-time host at the local Air Museum. It took only that long to decide that travel wasn't everything he'd dreamed. One year and he was ready to settle into an interesting, self-chosen occupation again. Travel brought too much discontinuity. A job restored life's stability.

You can see how the notion of *leisure-as-reward* puts work and leisure in false juxtaposition, the result being that both are misconceived. Properly seen, each exists for its own sake and both are meant to continue in a healthy and balanced symbiotic relationship.

One concern is this: care must be taken that as work was once an idol, so now leisure must not now become a substitute idol. Like all idols, this too would turn to emptiness. This needn't be the case, however, if free time is looked upon as providing opportunity to consider a range of occupational options—full or part-time, voluntary or compensated.

It's Your Choice

What leisure affords first and foremost is greater freedom of choice, a life open to unrestricted options, not the least of which involves new learning and different kinds of experience. Leisure enables us to *be* and *grow* and *do* as we desire. It affords opportunity for selecting what best serves our interests and needs.

We miss the point entirely if we fail to see leisure as *responsibility*—a new form of the stewardship of time and talent. And by stewardship we mean using something we possess for the purpose of fulfilling life-purposes.

As a new retiree, I concentrated first and foremost on the question of what would occupy my recreational leisure. I wanted to catch up on activities long deferred. Now was the time! Far less did I consider how I might take advantage of the opportunity to develop as a whole person and to let my life be one of freely given service. The faulty emphasis proved a great part of my ensuing disenchantment. I confess my mind-set was less than totally responsible and far too self-centered. Near-sighted vision is not a good way to tackle retirement! Neither is it a model of spiritual maturity. Retirement was meant for more than my own individual benefit.

Contrary to conventional wisdom, assimilation to the newly acquired leisure comes neither naturally nor automatically. Any number of things—many of which are psychological—can impede progress toward satisfactory adaptation. Studies at the University of California at Berkeley found, for example, that many retirees mourn their loss of regular employment the same as mourning the death of a loved one. Purely leisure activities cannot quench that grieving or satisfy the need to be meaningfully occupied.

As far back as 1929, Sigmund Freud in *Civilization and Its Discontents* noted that work "binds the individual more closely to reality [and] the human community." How true this is in our time. There's an unmistakable bond between work and human community. The opposite is equally true; absence of work acts *against* forming bonds with one's new community. So it is natural, then, that men and women are drawn to a continuing work experience to correlate with selected leisure pursuits. It may be for no better reason than building community with other retirees, all the while sharing occupational and service-oriented thinking and activity.

In a recent Sunday morning Bible class in our church, a man in his mid-80s told of the blessing and reward of ministering in a men's prison nearby. On another occasion someone spoke of working part-time in a thrift shop run by Christian organizations to support missions. Another, a former businessman and adjunct professor of business studies at Pepperdine University, is growing orchids on a commercial basis, something he had always wanted to do but couldn't afford to get started on his rather insufficient funds while at the same time holding down a full-time job. His hobby now became his occupation. As with others, he has joined that cheerful and optimistic group who love to report satisfying vocational activity.

The Biblical View of Retirement

Biblically, there is no logical foundation for the concept of total retirement from all work. As long as we're able, we're meant to be partners with Christ in the enterprise of Kingdom building, including world evangelism. God's enterprise on earth requires workers with a wide range of skills. Most importantly, it is a major way to please our Lord. Added to this, eternal rewards are based on our service for Christ.

Developing Strategies

Retirees who desire to combine leisure with meaningful self-occupation find they must make things happen for themselves. There can be no compulsion to engage in just anything for expediency's sake, or for pleasure's sake alone. Neither can retirees afford to be sold a bill of goods only to regret it later. To you I would say, think through how to make circumstances work *for* you, not *against* you. Now you have time to take greater control of your own life.

To help you serve these ends there are agencies prepared to help. These will be discussed later on.

If in this process any of us finds himself or herself somewhat adrift on an uncertain sea, we need not content ourselves by blaming circumstances. It may be our own inertia, apathy, lack of imagination, or absence of effort. If one or more of these turns out to be present, the problem is of our own making. So, to make our new situation what we want it to be, initially we need to adopt a thoughtful strategy, then take control of our circumstances. And except waiting upon God, there is little use to spend time waiting for some winning strategy to come our way. We must be proactive, reaching out, finding and seizing the God-directed opportunities. In this way we can discover a satisfactory combination of leisure with usefulness. In looking to God, we can move on with confidence. So don't put life on hold!

Misguided Expectations

Gerontologists agree that retired persons who have never learned along the way to determine the fundamental meaning of their lives are unlikely to organize their thinking sufficiently to find that meaning as they slip into retirement—certainly not quickly or without help. Montaigne had it right: "To retire successfully is no easy matter." Truly, for any of us to determine beforehand what's most important down the line—for instance, values to which we'll devote our final years—is no easy matter. Yet anticipating and planning need not be overly demanding—certainly not for individuals who for years have cultivated the habit of looking to God for guidance. Seeking His mind ought to be our continual practice, giving solid forethought as well as prayer to whatever our lives are meant to be in the future. Like it or not, planning is a necessary form of discipline. At its highest and best, it is a spiritually responsible exercise.

Moving Toward Maturity

Vienna psychologist Carl Jung dealt with this whole question, teaching that there are two turning points in every adult life. The first takes up the move from youthful years of occupational preparation to the period covered by working years. He emphasizes that during working years you learn to embrace a dual existence—combining career and family life. At a time when family development is crucial, it is career that tends to be uppermost. If a wife is also working, then in all likelihood economic well-being and status in the workplace generally win out.

The second turning point, Jung suggests, takes a person from career into what he calls "culture" (strange usage in English terminology). For Jung, "culture" is the final period of one's life span. There the focus turns to completing the process of personal maturity. No longer does the dual existence of career and family vie for first place, with career winning out. Now family life is fully established, children raised and gone, career goals now met, by and large. New horizons loom ahead. It is truly a turning point.

What Jung has in mind is the step beyond career, when one is free to develop individual personhood with all the exciting possibilities of an expanded and maturing personal life. This process, he says, follows an unquestioned law: human life is meant to move forward until no longer possible physically or mentally. Pragmatically, what anyone's personal life becomes is what that one makes it.

The Christian faces another dimension—God's leading. In the highest sense, retirement affords God's people great opportunity for knowing Him and His leading. The word *retirement* carries this disclaimer: it has far more to do with effective use of this special period of time than merely the cessation of salaried employment. It concerns no less than having an occupational activity that fulfills the person's deepest needs.

Jung, however, missed the whole message of the Christian faith. Little did he recognize this principle to be already present in Scripture, embedded in the larger subject of ongoing service to God with its hope of eternal reward.

Throughout his book *Psychology of the Spirit,* Jung says that for a person at this stage not to advance toward more complete human fulfillment is failure to see that not to acknowledge growing old is just as foolish as not wanting to leave one's childhood. Here Jung has in mind the reactivating of everything long sacrificed to career ends. To make it successfully in a career, the sacrifices required a large measure of organizational conformity—playing the world's game, being conventional man at his productive best. Now retired, the opportunity presents itself for a reawakening of everything newly placed within a person's grasp.

Under the pressures of career demands, working individuals are never able to break free to fully mature as persons—not, that is, until retirement forces upon them freedom's options. Then at last they have the chance to be, as Jung puts it, "an original," discovering "the values of personality." For the Christian, this is like receiving a clean slate to develop mature, self-fulfilling, Christian personhood. So, most importantly, the Christian can go on to become mature in the life Christ gives, infused with the essence of Christ's life and increasingly conformed to His likeness. It is as though God himself were set free to work out *His life* within the Christian's life. With no competing aspirations, there is freedom to concentrate upon life in Christ and follow His injunction: "Seek first the kingdom of God and His righteousness" (Matt. 6:33, NKJV). At long last, one is devoted to something higher—to the ultimate goal of becoming what God wants His child to be—a ministering servant living under the control and leading of the Spirit of God.

Use the new leisure for extended times of meditation on Scripture and prayer, for developing a quiet and unhurried deepened spirit. This is the time for learning obedience to the inner urgings of the Holy Spirit. You can also become an "unbound ambassador" to the world's needs, to seek the mind of Christ for ways to serve the cause of the gospel at home or on a broader field of world service. No longer do career obligations stand in the way. Why not consider short-term missions service abroad?

To chase down another problem, in our working years routine work demands tended to obscure any serious voids in our personal lives. Even when those voids were recognized, the tendency was to plunge relentlessly into our work in a subconscious attempt to blunt that awareness and ignore the need to make course corrections. In a sense, our work demands became an excuse for neglecting personal and family nurture. We "just didn't have time for everything," or so we thought and said.

Retirement, you see, forces us to measure personal success altogether differently than formerly. It is incumbent upon us to make our way through the Jungian second turning point, toward the completing of "maturity of the person," which means most of all spiritual maturity. If not a continuation of already established growth patterns, the need to grow in Christ ought now to take center stage. Psychologists following Jung's lead call this phase "interiorization"—finding latent qualities within the interior of the self, qualities not previously recognized, qualities subject to development in the present.

Internals for Externals

In our working years with the greatest deployment of talent and energy—peak years of achievement—we lived by and for the "externals," the outward symbols of vocational success and reward. But now the emphasis shifts to "internals"—to the interior life that represents the core of our true personhood. With the unique possibilities each personality possesses, externals should take a diminishing place while interior characteristics assume ascendancy. This goes along with turning from more formal relationships to those less formal and more personal and from obligatory work to chosen work to fulfill a higher purpose.

The importance of these matters is not lost upon contemporary psychologists. Roger L. Gould, writing in his early book *Transformations: Growth and Change in Adult Life,* concurs: "Our sense of meaning resides within us; it does not inhere in any extension of us that can be amputated by the wheel of fortune."[2]

As retired people we must learn to expect an emphasis on personal values that are no longer governed by things outside ourselves. We must learn to lead our own lives, not be led by external obligations, or pressures, or mere work rewards. We organize our own lives instead of letting them be organized for us, as was previously the case whether by the world of work or the culture that pressed upon us. Seriously, we must ask ourselves, are we prepared to take leadership over our own selves? Who or what will control our destiny? It's our call.

The option is ours: either we decide our own life-objectives and advance toward them, or default, fail to do this, and lose out. A worst-case scenario is to have our objectives dictated this time around by the have-a-good-time cult. For Christian men and women attuned to God's Spirit, such a course is not admissible. To *not* select your own retirement ideals, values, and occupations is self-defeating; it misses God's best. If you haven't done so, turn your choices over to Him!

It Is Self That Dignifies Work, Not the Reverse

It is mistaken but nonetheless natural to think that *do-ing* is more important than *being*—the very thing we did during working years. If work dignified self, most likely retirement activities ought to dignify self in similar fashion. It is, however, the exact reverse—*self dignifies work,* not the other way around. When we understand this we are relieved of concern that we must engage in replacement status building activities. As retirees, who we are in ourselves gives sufficient status to whatever it is we do.

These observations are exemplified by the retiree who couldn't tolerate losing in the senior bowling league, couldn't lay aside the competitive streak that had energized his business career. He's still geared to winning, still thinks he must win. But, really, does anything about retirement relate to winning? Or getting to the top? Oh, yes, perhaps the lawn bowling championship, or the blue ribbon at the orchid show, or even the bowling league. But it should be limited to "fun winning." From here on it is not about winning in occupational achievement. For the Christian, true "winning" applies to eternal rewards for faithful service for Christ our Lord, and the gratitude of those we help along life's way.

Communicating: The New Challenge

Paul Tournier makes this significant point: professional and business success depends on competence in one's field. Quite naturally this involves specialized communication, speaking the language of one's field of work. "Programmed" language develops between people who work together. What they do and how they talk about it brings about a commonality of communication and more connected relationships. People working together talk about the same things. But this has an undesirable effect as well. The discourse of personal relationships, however, is left quite severely undeveloped. Come retirement when we no longer relate through specialized work language, such bonding agents as shop talk cease to exist. A much broader basis for speech must take its place.

When we've retired and are outside former vocational circles, we may find we have little to talk about that fits the broader population of retirees. For instance, people don't want to hear discourses on what we've done, the nature of our job, who we've known, where we've been, when we had heart bypass surgery, who we voted for, or how long we've been an elder in the church. A little of that goes a long way. The danger lies in becoming ingrown, ending up talking to ourselves. So here we are, ripe in years but communication beginners again. Our former conversational skills haven't fully equipped us for building these new relationships.

We've all known people who engage others with merely superficial conversation, only to turn them off. They have nothing substantial to keep conversation inviting. We spot such people immediately, and, let's confess it, seek to avoid them. Little wonder we don't look forward to being with such individuals! The superficial is no substitute for the specialized; there must be a newly developed base of interests that broadens our conversational content. In time our former vocabulary shrinks and is replaced with more commonplace content. In the process we also learn to listen with a new pair of ears! So be on notice; there's no automatic way to shift from one set of conversational skills to another! This, too, is a new occupation. So get with it!

I've discovered it profitable to spend time in the public library with such journals as *Modern American History, Foreign Affairs,* and stimulating periodicals, such as *First Things.* As interests are enlarged, so conversation broadens and deepens. It is a good time to learn more about the world we live in and to be a more diversified conversationalist.

Another problem Tournier observes is that in our working years closely bonded relationships developed automatically, primarily because interpersonal communication was conducive to getting the job done, to reaching organizational targets that benefited everyone. So people worked together toward common ends. Relationships were, as sociologists say, "formal," aimed at smooth functioning. It was desirable that there be no intermixing of personal concerns. So whether they realized it or not, people came to relate to one another as "conversational functionaries." But what could be less personal, less satisfying in retirement, than being a "conversational functionary"!

When I left Westmont College faculty and colleagues, little did it occur to me that in retirement circles I would no longer be talking with sociologists, religious studies professors, faculty members, students, or other college personnel. Nor would I be conversing, as in earlier years, with pastors and denominational leaders. My new world included professionals from areas of expertise different from my own. Each were coming with his or her own particular interests to contribute. In their attempts to relate conversationally with me, or I with them, this was to be a problem. Certain areas of interest would have to be dropped on the part of each of us and new ones added in. I'd prefer to have avoided this, yet I knew it would be a life-enhancing experience, opening myself to desirable relationships. Every other retiree faced this problem to some degree; we were in the same boat together.

We who were together in the church could share core interests in the things of Christ; this was our common language, a common denominator. Our mutual faith and concern for the church's ministry in the world brought our active roles closer. Being with others in a Bible class widens the communication of everyone who attends. Should we not expect the church to be the Christian's rallying center, the integrating point for new relationships, new concerns, and service together with others?

When all is said and done, what a great advantage we have in spending our retirement years in the fellowship of like-minded Christians and having a core of spiritual concerns that can inform our conversations.

Retirees naturally hunger for personal relationships. Whether consciously or not, in one sense they are making up for relationships left behind. But most importantly, we seek social linkage of a kind superior to that which was promoted or even possible during work years. On the opposite end of the scale there are retirees who pursue this course too aggressively, attempting to achieve new friendships too quickly when this is best accomplished at a slower pace. As a slower pace may be best at the beginning, this leads some individuals to discouragement, or to withdrawal, as though this were a contest they were not winning. With more relaxed relationship-building these negative aspects can largely be avoided.

Retiring Isn't Retreating!

To retirees who think themselves failures in any respect, such as group acceptance, it's tempting to retreat inside themselves, to settle for an unnecessarily restricted lifestyle. To them, the very word "retire" sounds similar to "retreat," and to retreat is exactly what some people *do* when they think themselves failures.

I had a dear Christian friend whom I'd known since college days. While in his 60s, his wife died. He remarried soon thereafter, but the marriage didn't last. He had difficulty trying to become part of a Christian retired circle, feeling himself a virtual outcast because of the quick marriage and ensuing divorce—something he never envisioned happening to him. He began wandering from place to place, from friend to friend. He never profited from the support he might have had if only he'd given more effort to being a part of that Christian circle. He was unwilling to win that place. He just retreated, and his life was an unhappy one to the day he died several years later.

Do you see yourself retreating? Have you settled for the false image named "Failure"? Quit pouting and get moving; the outcome is really up to you! But you will have to work at it patiently, optimistically, and in earnest.

We *Are* Our Statuses

Commonly, although incorrectly, we hear the word *status* used in reference to prominence or prestige. A well-known figure is said to have status. This is not the way sociologists use the term. Rather, every person has status—in fact, more than a single status. Some individuals have many statuses. So what is status?

Status refers to your ranking in a social group, that is, your social standing or social recognition. Members of a group are ranked, some higher, some lower. This ranking differs from one group to another in which you participate. Some groups are small, say a family, others larger, say a business office or church fellowship. Since, generally, you belong to any number of groups, you will have more than one status—"statuses."

Statuses have an important bearing on our adjustment to retirement and in some cases bear on the psychological crisis many people experience. As a retiree, your statuses may change at various times in various situations. But whether your status is "ascribed," that is, assigned on the basis of certain fixed classifications, or achieved, based on the recognition of important accomplishments, it's important to realize that current statuses are no longer attached to our employment. Even though we tend to cling to those postrewarding statuses of our working years, we should realize that over time statuses change and status loss may trigger emotional troubles similar to those I experienced in my own retirement dilemmas.

Occupation 2

With a tinge of facetiousness, Simone de Beauvoir saw retirement adjustments as relatively easy for one particular segment of the population—those who throughout their lives had taken the road of mediocrity. These people will not have much difficulty fitting in. Since theirs was never much of a challenge to productive living, why should it be now? Retirement for them is freedom to follow their spontaneous impulses, to have "more fun, fewer responsibilities." Not growing to begin with, most likely they will not be growing now. In fact, personal growth may never have seriously interested them. People of mediocrity can be spotted rather easily and may be chalked off the list of "most qualified" to make the best companions in retirement. Not that they should be shunned; they might be helped. But how much more stimulating to know people intimately whose ideals are high and whose personal aspirations tend toward investing their retirement years in significant living.

For earnest Christians, retirement is certainly not meant for slouching into mediocrity. Commitment to Christ and His kingdom will inevitably elevate them above mediocrity at all stages of life. Since God has given them His best, they want to give Him their best. And since they have not been governed by mediocrity in their working years, life's strong objective remains that of making a valued contribution now more than ever before. Until we are incapacitated, all of us are meant to be active partners in His work. Retired laypeople need a vision of this from the start and local churches need to share the same vision with them, seeking out and inspiring retirees in their midst. It is here that churches have a valued resource to tap and a very natural way to extend the church's ministry. Across the board, peers relate to peers.

My own problem with retirement concerned how I might make a contribution that elevated daily routines and plans above such mediocrity. A mediocre use of time always troubled me. So the pressing question concerned what worthy and gratifying enterprise I could chose that would worthily occupy this final stretch of the road.

Page Smith makes the point that every life "should have its own unity and wholeness, its own form and integrity." Throughout a person's lifetime he or she may incorporate half a dozen careers or different phases of productivity. Each succeeding career change usually had some relation to those preceding it, a sense of continuity spanning the series of changes. In retirement it need not be all that different, save that not so much weighs on the change at this juncture of life.

This is Bob Buford's point in his book *Half-Time: Changing Your Game Plan from Success to Significance.* As a highly successful businessman, Buford reached midlife a millionaire only to want something besides success. Commitment to Christ brought him to see that life was meaningful only as it was lived significantly. For Buford it meant using the same skills employed in business to be a consultant to Christian organizations that could profit from better managerial skills. His story serves to show how some retirees can transfer over their long-developed skills to their new retirement occupation.

Some experts are calling retirement "an arbitrary intervention in a person's ongoing life." There is a real point to this insight as we note the discontinuity retirement so often creates. That discontinuity is lessened when a vocation is found that is congruous with the background of work from which a person has come. The adjustment is lessened.

The way we think about life as a whole can be distorted if we assume that retirement is not to be considered an extension of our past history. Instead of having coherence and continuity, our lives are in danger of unnecessarily being reduced to divided personal narratives. What we consider "good" experience is always an asset. Still, it should be emphasized that past experience is not a necessary requisite for building a retirement vocation. At best it makes for fewer adjustments.

"Free-choice" or "new life" vocation is chosen not out of necessity but solely because it meets three criteria: It is interesting, has objectives worthy of full-hearted participation, and meets the individual's need for a newly acquired lifestyle that honors God. To this end retirees need to devote full thought and energy to projects socially and spiritually meaningful. At the same time the choice should not place a person under a sense of obligation or stress.

Committed to God's Leading

To make time count meaningfully involves finding and choosing a specific occupation with the assurance of God's leading, then committing oneself to it. It should not be either one of two extremes—*time-filling* or *time-restricting*. The choice is best based on needs and goals unrelated to economic needs or desires.

Fundamentally, free-choice vocations are motivated by purposes that rise above self-aggrandizement. At the very heart is an intrinsic social benefit that beckons enthusiastic participation. Working associations are to be more like social relationships—a far cry from interactions to promote corporate or professional goals. More than "getting along harmoniously," it carries the expectation of a high degree of ongoing personal satisfaction.

We're not thinking, you see, about an economic undertaking as such, or about nice ways to "keep mind and body busy." Rather, it is response to an inner call for quality existence—the meaningful use of time, thought, energy, and resources. Goals include maturing as God's man or woman and reaching out helpfully to other lives, making a difference in the quality of life around ourselves.

A special aspect of Christian free-choice vocations is the place for spontaneity and imagination, for vocations governed more by what is creative than contracted as is typical of the business and professional world. For these reasons "free-choice" occupations are "freeing" to the spirit, to be embraced with joyousness. The key terms are *stress-free, joyousness, service*—"serving *God* through serving *people.*"

All this is not to say free-choice vocations cannot be financially profitable; not at all. My retirement occupation, for example, is research and writing—serving the Lord through the printed page, a direct carryover from a former multifaceted career. Although I'm no longer a pastor or professor, I fulfill this part of my former self-definition—"Christian writer." Of course, where there is opportunity to teach God's Word, to offer spiritual counsel, or to step in as a volunteer in a church project, I serve God in those free-choices as well. Because of health limitations some avenues would be burdensome, so necessarily limited. Here again, is not this also fully within God's direction? Along with a modest retirement subsistence, my writing income, while not great, is most welcome. But the point is that compensation is neither the primary motivation nor the ultimate satisfaction. It is best when there is no compelling association between earning money and personal satisfaction. The more important objective is to make a contribution to people's lives, and if there is some measure of remuneration, that's an added benefit to be prayerfully incorporated into my stewardship of the "all things" received from God's gracious hand and returned to Him in one form or another. Of course, for persons who need additional income to provide a decent quality retirement, understandably that must factor in.

About such vocations, Paul Tournier asserts that this reconversion to the second, retirement career implies an equally important inner conversion. If there remains an obsessive secret nostalgia for the old order of things, then that must frankly be recognized as an obstacle to the very nature of free-choice vocation. The retired person must be free in mind to construct a new future.[3]

Equally pertinent is Tournier's word: "If one dwells on one's past working life, either regretting it or complaining about it, going back to it in thought and spirit when one can no longer return to it in reality, one drains the present of its color, and deprives oneself of the joys that may be found in a second career."[4]

So far as possible, the vocation one chooses should be free from causing stress to either physical or emotional health, although, to be sure, a moderate output of physical and emotional energy is to be expected.

Free-choice vocation should also be relatively free from drudgery. Not that every aspect of one's chosen task will be stimulating, fulfilling, or completely drudgery-free. It is the easily-recognized overload that will cause difficulty.

Additionally, chosen occupations must have intrinsic worth, that is, value simply in the doing. It goes without saying that there ought also to be a sense of something accomplished capable of lifting one's own spirit as well as benefiting others. Where the task is right and one is assured of God's leading, the inner satisfaction will surely transcend any elements considered humdrum or less than challenging.

When Ruth and I retired and moved to San Jose, the pastor of the church I had pastored many years before invited me to minister to seniors. I took this on as a noncompensated volunteer position and loved what I was doing. I had no problem working under another pastor who was considerably younger than I. So for the time this arrangement was right. The time did come when I had to realize that task-related stresses were becoming greater than desired, and so gave up the position. My decision had nothing to do with another man in authority or with any relational or institutional problems, but solely with the demands on time, energy, and health.

Can Another's Authority Be a Problem?

Sometimes, in a free-choice occupation there does lurk an unforeseen problem of authority. Retirees may find themselves placed within a hierarchy where other persons are over them. For many professional or business people this is perfectly acceptable, no cause for distress. For others it is difficult. Take the case where the vocation freely chosen is found to fulfill nearly all of a person's expectations but is stressful because another individual's authority is cause for chafing. This occupation may not be the best choice. The opposite scenario is possible too. If one takes a volunteer position that requires authority over others, this may cause stress as well. So if authority issues induce undesirable stress, for either reason just mentioned, one should pray about abandoning the job for something else. To leave is not to be a dropout or a quitter. Maybe it's just being wise enough to know when something isn't going to work out and so shouldn't be continued under the pretense that the problem will go away if we just ignore it. A person can always back out graciously and accept it as his or her own problem, not necessarily the problem of the one in authority.

Certainly, negative factors, such as problems of authority, need not suggest closure to all similar possibilities. Similarly, if coworkers with lesser competence hinder the retiree's capacity to continue as a positive worker, this too may indicate it is not God's will to stay. It all boils down to how well one can adapt.

It's OK to Experiment

Retirement careers are often a matter of willingness to give something a try, testing whether it is right or not, then either settling in or moving on to something else. In trying different routes that might prove only temporary, there isn't the same high-stakes that tended to prove threatening in the working world. The retiree isn't making the same investment of self in the compulsion to succeed. No corporate ladder beckons, no fellow employees are competing or evaluating one's every move. The retiree isn't pressured to prove himself or herself. Nor are they trying to make a personal statement other than willingness to serve. The challenge is simply to give the new role a try and find what is best for oneself. God will make it known, and it may prove reassuring to have tried more than one possibility before finding what is best.

In search of the new vocation, there's no reason not to pursue various possibilities. Time isn't pressing, nor does the final choice need to be settled at once. Nothing this time around should threaten your present or future welfare. Of the many existing opportunities, there are always ways of learning how to qualify at the desired level.

Marlow Dannenbring regularly ministers to convicts in the Men's Colony just outside San Luis Obispo (a minimum security prison). The men love Marlow for his caring spirit and readiness to spend time with them on a one-to-one basis. He is known not to be partial to certain inmates, but ministers to all alike. He is like a father to many men. Joyfully, he reports to our Bible class about men who have come to Christ, men who know him to be a completely authentic and humble Christian servant whose witness is backed up by his life. Marlow's desire to honor his Savior is a vital inspiration. He is wisely and joyfully investing his life in retirement for God.

So often what creates and sustains a new interest is the association with a new group of people—people, it turns out, well worth knowing. Since first impressions are often deceiving, it takes time to feel comfortable with people we've known only a short while. They, too, may be feeling their own way with a degree of uncertainty. All the more must we expect to nurture these new contacts both for their sakes and ours, giving the process time to develop.

What we're commending is willingness to explore a broad range of possibilities, ruling out none, then taking the plunge and patiently giving the new opportunity reasonable time to develop. At first thought, a volunteer position may seem out of character, yet once experienced it becomes highly attractive and perfectly *in* character. Consciously looking to God to indicate His choice is the way of Christian faith. God always honors faith.

Don't Get Impatient

Along with natural anxiety when facing an uncertain future, or when trying out what may not be the eventual occupation, there is the tendency for "doers" to succumb to impatience. Used to seeing things done promptly and expeditiously but now having to go through a period of experimentation your patience is tried. You may be surprised to find that the patience you had in former years is less now—not uncommon to the aging process. Then, too, patience sometimes has to be learned under a new set of conditions. With God's enablement it can be achieved.

At times when I've been impatient there comes to mind a moving story told by Nikos Kazantzakis.

> I remember one morning when I discovered a cocoon in the bark of a tree, just as the butterfly was making a hole in its case and preparing to come out. I waited awhile, but it was too long appearing and I was impatient. I bent over it and breathed on it to warm it. I warmed it as quickly as I could and the miracle began to happen before my eyes, faster than life. The case opened, the butterfly started slowly crawling out and I shall never forget my horror when I saw how its wings were folded back and crumpled; the wretched butterfly tried with its whole trembling body to unfold them. Bending over it, I tried to help it with my breath. In vain. It needed to be hatched out patiently, and the unfolding of the wings should be a gradual process in the sun. Now, it was too late. My breath had forced the butterfly to appear all crumpled before its time. It struggled desperately and, a few seconds later, died in the palm of my hand.[5]

Is it not a common temptation to try to "help God" unfold His plan by intruding our own "helpfulness"? The sad consequence is that we thereby destroy the very opportunity God wants to place before us. I like Kazantzakis's thoughtful conclusion: "We should not hurry, we should not be impatient, but we should confidently obey the eternal rhythm."[6]

God works within the "eternal rhythm" He has ordained. But the need *He sees* may not be the same need *we see*. So our part is to learn to wait upon Him and not impatiently flail around on our own. He will direct the waiting spirit. *Just trust Him!*

Does Fear Overcome You?

Together with the uncertainty of finding our place as retirees, and with a natural impatience to get life resettled on a routine track once more, there may be a rising fear of not succeeding, of not doing well, of not looking good in the eyes of others. *Shades of the past!* How inhibiting such fears can be! You may have been long-settled in your career and therefore forgotten what it was like when you had to prove yourself, work your way up, gain self-confidence and acceptance among your associates. Now old questions reappear—questions of qualifying for the task or of being accepted by the group. This resistance to move *out* in order to move *on* is fully understandable. But it must be reversed.

Inertia is another problem that can hold back retirees. The longer a person waits to move ahead, the greater the inertia that must be overcome. Now is the time the cycle of passivity and natural reluctance must be broken—and the sooner the better.

Accept Encouragement from Others

Being together with successful retirees, you soon discover how typical it is to explore various occupational avenues, tentatively move ahead, make mistakes, try second and third times, and perhaps have a few laughs about misadventures. Finally the right course appears and, yes indeed, all along God had His appointed solution. When we've arrived at that place, we can appreciate the process we've gone through and the lessons God had for us along the way. He knew what He was doing!

When you eventually find your "place," you feel reinstated in the flow of life and soon settle in. Self-confidence quickly returns. Forging new social linkages and undertaking something never before attempted makes it a stimulating new experience. We feel good when a challenge has been met successfully. The right free-choice vocation provides the reward of going farther than first expected. It is a stretching experience guaranteed to bring genuine growth, besides being useful and satisfying.

Our Need to Be Esteemed

We all have the need to be esteemed by others for just who we are in ourselves. This has a lot to do with how we value ourselves. Looking back, most of us valued ourselves for our career accomplishments. Others valued us for the same reasons, and we appreciated their valuation. As retirees we need a new basis for self-valuation. We want to know who we are in ourselves as persons, totally apart from anything that makes up our circumstances. This will come about through deciding the quality of life we want, through attention to personal relationships, and through activities that bring about greater human fulfillment. Such an achievement usually calls for major reconstruction of personal habits including that of reaching out to people.

Viktor Frankl of Vienna, father of the psychology known as *logotherapy*, finds cause for neuroses in the retirement crisis—calling it "unemployment neurosis." Others since Frankl see such ill-effects as disease and physical degeneration resulting from "retirement malaise." It is an accepted premise today that whatever the causal factors, when retirees fail to attain a genuine measure of growth, fail to have a solid sense of life's ultimate meaning, there may indeed develop both physical and emotional dysfunction. For this reason we are examining the connection between psychological, social, and spiritual health. The three go together in terms of wholeness of personality.

More than ever before, Americans aged 65 to 74—peak retirement years—are volunteering for community service or are helping others with a great variety of needs. Interestingly, this significant increase has occurred in one generation. *May it continue!*

There are a multitude of places where a person can make a difference through service to others in the name of Christ, places where their faith will make a definite impact. Community activities and volunteer service projects are among the most available and congenial.

Community activities run the gamut from health care to social services, special education, the arts, and various forms of social advocacy. Community services provide assistance to the elderly and handicapped, to disadvantaged youth, the homeless and indigent. Volunteers renovate dilapidated apartments and build low-cost housing. Tens of thousands of the adult population volunteer their services in public-supported hospitals and clinics, many of which are located in low-income areas of inner cities. Thousands of citizens serve as big brothers and sisters in single-parent households. Many others serve in daycare centers and in after-school programs to assist working mothers. Some provide counseling for runaways and troubled youth or serve as English tutors for non-English speaking adults. A growing number of people volunteer in crisis centers for pregnant teens or for victims of spouse or child abuse, while still others work in drug rehabilitation centers. Thousands staff public shelters and assist in the distribution of clothes and food to the needy and the housebound. Retired professionals—lawyers, doctors, accountants, executives, teachers—donate time pro bono in a host of existing programs that require their special professional expertise and credentials. And then there are environmental projects, recycling, and conservation programs. A significant number work for advocacy organizations attempting to redress grievances, to change discriminatory public perceptions or on behalf of constituencies whose interests are either being ignored or underrepresented. Some choose crime prevention work or disaster relief. These are the unsung heroes of our time. They seldom get the headlines, but they are "headliners"!

The opportunities are limitless for individuals who are independent of economic demands and willing and able to move into some new sector of life. When people volunteer to serve others, in whatever way it is expressed, a climate is created where those volunteers often have a great personal reception from the beneficiaries. Frequently they find hearts open to a witness for Christ and His motivating love. The demonstration of Christian caring has preceded the spoken word. In these ways, working with other people in similar services, in what now is a true peer group of retirees, extraordinary opportunities are provided for Christian example and witness.

Retirees who work part-time in what is called "social sector organizations" help make possible the economic vitality of the nation, although they represent just 9 percent of the total national employment. The importance is recognized when it is seen that the assets of social sector organizations by 1995 equaled nearly half the assets of the federal government.[7]

A 1991 Gallup survey revealed that more than 94 million adult Americans, or 51 percent of the population, gave time to various causes and organizations. The average volunteer gave 4.2 hours of his or her time per week. Collectively, the American people gave more than 20 billion hours volunteering, an economic contribution equivalent to 9 million full-time employees. If measured in dollars, it would be worth $176 billion. Who says we retirees aren't a generous bunch? Does all this give you some ideas?

There are multiplied thousands of nonprofit organizations in the United States whose primary goals are to provide services or advance causes. They are located in every American community. Such community service is a revolutionary alternative to traditional forms of labor. It is neither coerced nor based on a fiduciary relationship. Instead, it is a helping action, reaching out to others. Here personal labor is entered into willingly and usually without expectation of material gain. It is motivated by a personal sense of indebtedness for their own blessings and a desire to serve. This attitude makes for an entirely different kind of worker. We can see readily that free-choice vocation wonderfully fits Christian idealism. It can be a bouquet of life to the Lord.

In what manner do we—you and I—respond to the debt we owe the Savior in serving others whom He loves? What better demonstration of Christian servanthood? What better representation of the Master? And what better way to find joy in what we do! The Lord wants to place us where He is able to provide that joy.

Clearly, these benefits require personal commitments. And here the challenge is to raise the level of the church body to a more compassionate, more caring human community. And it is in the church fellowship that individuals can encourage and help each other find their places of service.

Shouldn't Christians be leading the way? Do able, healthy retired Christians have any excuse not to be involved? I continually ask this of myself. And what about you? Have you brought this to the Lord in prayer? Are you ready to step out with a servant heart? If you are, the Lord will not leave you without making clear His open doors.

Showing the Way

Recently the monthly alumni magazine of my alma mater, the University of California, arrived. The issue interviewed the alumnus of the year, Dr. Marian Diamond, a world-renowned professor of integrative biology. Vibrant and energetic at age 70, Diamond said she had no plans to retire in the foreseeable future. In her words, "There is so much to learn. Someone recently asked to write a book about my life. I said, 'You can't do that. I've hardly begun to live!'"

Rex Tyner is an active, southern California layman, who retired at age 69 as a superintendent of schools. Interested in gerontology, he became a trained lecturer on this subject. Now 86 years young, he cohosts a TV program, *Senior Scene*, in San Clemente, California, and lectures in a healthcare center on current interests relating to gerontology. It keeps his mind young and energizes his active participation in a vibrant lifestyle.

Who says we retirees can't move on to higher planes of personal influence? So often a happy and fulfilled life in retirement begins with commitment to something new and creative. It succeeds in getting retirees' eyes off themselves and counters the negatives that tend to rob life of its vitality. Retirement is the new staging ground for undreamed-of creativity. Retirees are not limited by age, only by the reach of their imaginations and prudent use of their gifts.

"As for every man to whom God has given riches and wealth, and given him power to eat of it, to receive his heritage and rejoice in his labor—this is the gift of God. For he will not dwell unduly on the days of his life, because God keeps him busy with the joy of his heart" (Eccles. 5:19-20, NKJV).

6

Feeling Unfinished
and Unfulfilled

Paul Tournier says that none of us ever comes to the place where career success or the development of personhood can assure complete human fulfillment. Realistically, we ought not to expect it. In a splendid chapter on acceptance, he writes:

"The particular acceptance I am referring to here is perhaps one of the most difficult to achieve; it is acceptance of unfulfillment. That is one of the great problems of retirement, among many the toughest to face up to. Professional or business life is over, and it has 'finished the yet unfinished.'"[1]

Our task is to take in stride and cope with "acceptance of the unfulfilled." Or, as we are calling it, "the unfinished." How do we meet the dilemma of the unfinished?

Some of us have been driven by unrealistic expectations and a competitive nature since high school or college days. When occupational pursuits are past, we trouble over unrecoverable lost opportunities with unfulfilled goals and unrealized relationships. This, in other words, is *the dilemma of the unfinished.* We agonize, "Do I have to leave things unfinished? Something is missing from my long years of work."

This incompleteness rests as a curse. All those working years the dream was of getting to the top. But it was never reached. Now time is gone, opportunity lost. It becomes an agonizing question: "Why does our time here have to end with so much left unfinished?" Not just the end of work achievements, but the end of life itself haunts the sensitive, thoughtful spirit. The unfinished becomes a prefiguration of death—the end-point of all earth's unfinished business. In Roger Mehl's terse word, retirement brings "an end, but not a fulfillment."

Different from previous adult transitions, retirement brings with it this ominous sense of finality. For non-Christians there is the uncertainty of what lies beyond life as they know it. With uncertainty comes thoughtfulness, but thoughtfulness breeds fear. For Christians, while the unfinished and the unfulfilled are difficult to accept, the prospect of a completely fulfilled life in heaven beckons ever more brightly. So God's people may be more satisfied here.

Rather than try to cope with such a fearful prospect, many non-Christians engage in meaningless busyness. They "dance the night away." Others deteriorate rapidly in health or mental acuity. Fearing the end of life, they give up on life. How unspeakably sad!

For the person who demands optimal personal fulfillment in the here and now, the approaching end carries the same fear. The record of past successes and joys is dimmed by the looming expectation of the end of all things earthly—even their best memories. Everything past and present fades in significance.

So death can be a time when all unfulfilled hopes are dashed forever, when what is unfinished will remain forever unfinished. Or in stark contrast, death can be birth into life eternal, signifying a fresh beginning in heaven with nothing unfinished. While keeping eternity's values in view, the Christian can use the remaining time to serve the Lord without this overburdening concern.

In this interim retirement period characterized by the increasing limitations of age, there is assurance that whatever God expects of us is achievable with the strength He gives. Age and time are not factors standing in the way. We are stewards of all God gives us, including strength for the last period of time He allots us. He asks only that we be good stewards, faithful servants, Christlike disciples.

With sufficient financial assets, reasonably good health, and a busy lifestyle, it's not difficult to dismiss thoughts of the finality of everything they're engaged in now. Roger Gould says, "As though there was a pact with the world: if we worked hard and succeeded and made proper sacrifices along the way, we would be annihilated one day. Work enabled us to sanitize the fear of our own mortality."[2]

Do you have eternity's values in view? Interestingly, individuals with a denial mind-set often have no plans to retire—ever. It's as though by continuing whatever they are now engaged in they are granted immunity from having to face the end of all things earthly, including their own life. But can they escape forever the ultimate questions about the meaning of life's end? How will the pains of grief or a hospital bed or an unwanted prognosis affect such denial?

It's an illusion. The continuation of working symbolically represents the continuation of the power to live on. "Person at work" it says, as though the continuation of work routines gives the power to live on. *What an illusion!*

When you reach retirement, one thing is certain whether it enters your thinking or not: the final period of life has been entered, the final lap, the final earthly opportunity. At some moment—be it far or near, and often unexpectedly—each person will cross into eternity. Necessarily, then, we must ask what remains to transfer over there? The Bible will give us that answer.

One reason we struggle against the unfulfilled and the unfinished is our tendency to view this phenomenon in the category of personal failure. But how mistaken to equate success with tasks completed, failure with tasks not completed.

So how are we going to deal with what's left unfinished, we who know the Lord? Christians should look at the apostle Paul as their example. When he reached the finish of his ministry he could say,

> As for me, I feel the last drops of my life are being poured out for God. The time for my departure has arrived. The glorious fight that God gave me I have fought, the course I was set I have finished, and I have kept the faith. The future holds for me the crown of righteousness which the Lord, the true judge, will give to me in that day—and not, of course, only to me but to all those who have loved what they have seen of him *(2 Tim. 4:6-8, PHILLIPS)*.

To life's end, Paul invested everything for the kingdom of God. His life was a ministry wherever he was and under whatever circumstances. Still, in human terms, not all of it was successful, not every mission was completed. His life drew near its end in a prison where he knew death awaited him. But even there, some of his most precious and positive thoughts, his most glorious teaching, come to us from his confinement. In his prison letter to the church at Philippi, he urges all believers to learn the life of rejoicing, even as he himself is overjoyed with his status and hope in Christ: "For to me, to live is Christ and to die is gain" (1:21, NIV).

There is no indication that the unfinished could deter the great apostle from his ultimate joy. With one foot planted on earth and the other in heaven, the meaning of his personal being was firmly established in the life of eternity. He was totally unconcerned with what he considered an unfinished ministry. His joy was that others were coming along to take it up—like young Timothy, his son in the faith. As for himself, his own times were in God's hands. There was nothing to fear. Whenever he would be called to pass the mantle to others, it would be the right time; God was in control of all things, and He makes no mistakes!

The Christian should not look upon retirement as the end of living—life's last phase. We are all moving toward an "end," but only an earthly end. To use Paul's term, we are preparing for "departure time," looking to the kingdom of God and eternal residence with the Lord and with all the redeemed people of God from every age. There is full awareness of the scripture that says, "For here we have no lasting city, but we seek the city which is to come" (Heb. 13:14). So Paul could look with no regrets beyond any disappointments, beyond all unfinished tasks. His personal growth, much like victory over sin and self-centeredness, was only partially realized. But he rejoiced in the prospect of being made whole in Christ in the life to come and looked ahead to serving Him forever. So as long as life continued, he wished only to be a positive witness to his Lord's grace and goodness, and to be content to "do the doable."

Is this not great enough incentive to the Christian retiree who wants more than anything to live a life that counts? Joyousness comes with the sense that there are still gifts of labor and love to lay at the Savior's feet.

Viktor Frankl stressed the place of meaning in a person's life. "Deep within himself," he wrote, "man seeks a meaning for his life, and tries to fulfill himself in accordance with that meaning."[3] The task is to know for sure where the highest meaning is found. No human counselor or sage can supply the answer, but the God of heaven can and does! Retirement is a time to become immersed in God's Word as never before.

Healing Unfinished Relationships

Unfinished relationships seem to overtake us in retirement. That includes those severed by death, divorce, alienation, or perhaps a distant move away from cherished friends. With time now to contemplate the loss in clearer light, it's easier to see what requires attention. It may be a relationship that needs mending or one that needs to be refocused and deepened. Recovering or repairing a relationship can prove to be a major advance toward personal fulfillment—a noble retirement occupation!

When a dear one dies—as so often occurs during retirement years—one of life's most cherished relationships is left seemingly incomplete. For non-Christians, what dawns with such force is that all human attachments are left uncompleted, making closure so difficult. But for Christians there is the blessed hope of personal reunions in heaven. There all human bonds, though not the same as on earth, will continue in the perfect sense in which God designed them. Again, God completes all good things that we leave incomplete.

Others besides Frankl have found that such ill effects as disease and physical degeneration result from retirement malaise. It is well established that life and health are closely bound up with these two things: *(a)* a sense of personal fulfillment, and *(b)* whether or not life continues to be meaningful.

Saying Yes to God

Accepting the unfulfilled and the unfinished as normal expectations and moving on to employ retirement wisely is to say "Yes" to all we receive from God's hand. Let me illustrate.

Dr. E. Stanley Jones, late world Christian statesman and evangelist to many lands, wrote a helpful little book with the aid of his daughter and her husband when he was in his late 80s and physically impaired. The book, last of many, was titled *The Divine Yes*.[4]

Jones tells a story that has some parallels with my own, perhaps yours as well. He recounts a conversation with a retired Methodist bishop who was restless and frustrated. Whether the bishop fully recognized it or not, what troubled him was no longer being a well-recognized person, no longer publicly prominent. Conscious of a need, his question to Dr. Jones had to do with knowing the secret of victorious living at such a time as this.

"It is," said Jones, "in self-surrender, in giving up the innermost self to Jesus." The problem, Jones pointed out, was in the texture of the things that held his bishop friend. When the outer strands were broken by retirement, the inner strands were not enough to hold him. Then Jones gave his own witness to the truth of what he was talking about. At age 87, he had a stroke and was consigned to living with insurmountable handicaps—impairment of vision, hearing, speech, locomotion, use of one arm. (This was in 1971. He was to live for 14 months in this condition). "The glorious thing was that my faith was not shattered. I was not holding it; it was holding me." To the bishop, Jones pointed out that when in his own life the outer strands were cut by this stroke, life didn't shake because it was held by the inner strands. His message: "When we don't possess faith, faith possesses us. When we seem not to possess God, He possesses us! When life is shouting a human 'No,' there is a Divine 'Yes' that resounds even louder!"

Just before he died at age 89, Jones gave this final testimony: "I can't afford to be anything but grateful that He thought enough of me to give me this period at the end of life to be a proof that what I've spoken about—the unshakeable Kingdom and the unchanging Person—is true because I'm showing it to be true by His grace."[5]

We needn't spell retirement as though it equates with resignation into apathy and disinterest. It cannot be mere

assent to "what life now affords." These are passive responses, none of them really saying "Yes." Acceptance is
active response—or to adopt Paul Ricoeur's term, "active
personal surrender." In E. Stanley Jones's word, it is "giving up the innermost life to Jesus."

When we closely associate "active" with "surrender," as
Ricoeur does, are we combining opposites? I think not. Surrender is actively giving oneself over to something or to
someone. To do so gladly and meaningfully is to take the
initiative, actively and committedly taking on whatever
we're giving ourselves to. Acceptance also implies redirec-
tion—not necessarily moving toward something "less," perhaps only "different." Here is acceptance and affirmation at
its finest and fullest, letting God make known His perfect
plan for this time of life and answering the divine yes with
the human yes. In retirement we come much closer to that
acceptance, more ready to say "yes," to making an active
surrender to its inevitability. It should be a time of joyful
anticipation.

In searching for the meaning of death, the German
philosopher Heidegger saw it as interrupting life and making life incomplete, but said that incompleteness is a con-
stituent of our being and death teaches us that life is a value, but an incomplete value. He was wrong insofar as he
looked only at this side of the grave and not beyond. Heidegger was unable to see life's incompleteness as something completed in eternity with God. We who are Christ's
can accept incompleteness now because it leads to the ultimate completion! I want to make important preparation
now in these retirement years. How about you?

Michael Cassidy's *The Passing Summer* is a policy approach to the agony of South Africa during apartheid—
black rage and white fear. It is also about the politics of
love. In the final chapter titled "No Continuing City," he

writes, "For if we do not live under the aspect of eternity, we will be corrupted into thinking that earth is our home."[6] Cassidy includes a quotation from C. S. Lewis, who wrote in *God in the Dock* that "If men indeed exist for the glory of God, then their final end and their destiny as persons is not to be found in this passing world."[7]

Sometimes the feeling of futility in retirement lies in trying "to feel at home in this world." Retirement might better be a time when we wean ourselves from assuming that our destiny resides in anything realized in this passing world. How truly Goethe observed that "those who do not hope for another life are always dead to this one." The Christian's hope in Christ keeps the spirit alive through every change, through every dark foreboding! What may seem so uncertain takes on certainty through faith in the One who plans the whole of our lives for time and for eternity. Our strategy lies in taking each day as He gives it, and in giving Him day-by-day control.

Just because we come to realize our true home is not this passing world, does this world then become a less interesting place in which to live for the present? Is there less reason to give attention to what God is doing in His world? Have we retired from utilizing a healthy curiosity? Have we renounced appreciation for all He's blessed us with in the surrounding beauty of this world? Shouldn't our interests embrace as much of His world as possible, right up to our leaving it for the next? (See Rom. 8:19-22 and Rev. 21—22.) I tend to "turn off" what is happening in the world as though I don't need to have an interest in what I soon will leave behind. But this, of course, only diminishes my sharpness about so much that should continue to make life valuable. Are you tempted in this same direction?

Even though many retirees have financial means and health to travel abroad, they fail to see the wonders of His hand in the great diversity that makes up His world. Still others with very limited mobility who can travel little, if at all, are enthralled with the wonders they observe all around them. It's a difference in outlook, and it is our outlook that colors all of life, especially in the waning years.

Which type of person will you be? It's all there—but only in the eye of the beholder, in the observation of a person alive in spirit, one who remains vibrant and curious. Recalling the old adage, "Take time to smell the roses," we are the richer if in these our retirement years we take that time. Our understanding and enjoyment of God is enhanced as we contemplate the wonders and beauties of His creation.

The freedom we gain in retirement is freedom to exercise a maturing personal power as never before. It has nothing at all to do with power in the workplace—organizational, social, economic, or political power—the same power that once resided in title, position, rank, or prominence. Neither is it the power of former times in the company of influential people. It has solely to do with power to be the person God wants us to be—power to grow and advance in spiritual life as part of His family. It is inner power—power from God through His Spirit, power to live positively, joyfully, and fruitfully. It is power to fulfill God's best in our inner being, in our relationships, in our service. That's power as God intended power to be!

Toward Maturity

Retirement should find us advancing along an ever-increasing maturity—both spiritually and socially. Included in that growth should be a broader mind, deeper spirit, and wider understanding of the world we inhabit with all its needs and sorrows. We should be maturing in loving compassion as we grasp what God is doing in our time both in His church and among the lost.

I have a retired friend who will not look at anything in the newspaper or on television depicting the tragic needs in the world. He says it's all too sad, and he does not want his mind to be filled with negative images. But should we not, all of us, be maturing in compassion as we know the world's needs, seeking to be comforters even as God comforts us? Do we need to hide our eyes from that which God may use to call us to a compassionate ministry as our occupation in these days of freedom to serve Him? Do we not have time for a more compassionate prayer ministry if nothing else?

There's the mistaken notion that retirement is the end of having definite goals to drive our lives forward, no longer anything to struggle for, to aspire toward—no particular ends we must concentrate our efforts to attain. But then, what better way to lose life's vitality, to be cheated of some special fulfillments! Provisional and tentative though some goals necessarily have to be, they are genuinely meant to activate us toward reaching beyond ourselves and in the process to exercise a whole new vitality to reverse some of the currents of a decadent culture that drags life down.

So for all the unfinished matters we have to leave finished, we have a splendid word from Frances de Sales: "It is right that you should begin again every day. There is no better way to finish the spiritual life than to be ever beginning."

As the apostle Paul considered the high calling of God in Christ Jesus and the eternal reward that would compensate every relinquishment and pain suffered in this world, he took pen in hand and wrote his beloved friends in Philippi of his determination to leave the past behind, and looking ahead, set his sights on the goal of all goals:

"I forget all that lies behind me and with hands out-

stretched to whatever lies ahead I go straight for the goal—
my reward the honour of my high calling by God in Christ
Jesus" (Phil. 3:13-14, PHILLIPS).

When Years Draw Long

Some retirees are limited by age, perhaps severely limited. Night is fast encroaching. The apostle Paul challenges
them as he does us: "I can do all things through Christ who
strengthens me" (Phil. 4:13, NKJV). He didn't add, "except
when I'm over 65."

If in the eternal habitations the best is yet to be, the encroaching night is only the harbinger of that day "which
breaks eternal bright and fair." Whatever losses we sustain
as we grow older and our powers are diminished, recall another word of the apostle Paul to the Philippian church, "I
count all things to be loss in view of the surpassing value
of knowing Christ Jesus my Lord" (3:8). This is a challenge
for any age retiree.

A Man to Remember

The Bible records the story of a great overcomer with
whom older retirees can relate since his greatest days were
in his old age: Caleb (see Josh. 14—15).

God said of Caleb, "[He] has followed me fully" (Num.
14:24). Moses gave identical testimony, saying that he
"wholly followed the LORD my God" (Josh. 14:9). Caleb
himself affirmed this to be true: "I wholly followed the LORD
my God" (v. 8). Here was a candidate for divine blessing!

Caleb was not an Abraham or a Moses, neither a David
nor a Paul. He was just a man among men, ordinary in
many respects yet living an extraordinary life. There's no
record of fame. His life was extraordinary because of his re-

lationship to God in whom he placed his utmost confidence—a relationship of unswerving faith and total obedience. But at 85 he wasn't through yet.

Choosing the Faith Way

God had chosen a people for himself and promised them a special land, Canaan, for their everlasting possession. During Caleb's time, they were at the very gates. God invited them to possess it as His gift, yet instructed them that they must take it by force, promising that He would enable them in the conquest (see Num. 13—14).

God had already told the people that the nations presently occupying the land were mightier than they but promised to go before them and drive their enemies from the land. They were to be of good courage.

Caleb was 1 of the 12 chosen to spy out the land. Ten of them reported insurmountable difficulties, but Joshua and Caleb magnified the power of the Lord to overcome those difficulties. Their verdict was unhesitating.

Caleb, acting as the spokesman, said, "Let us go up at once and occupy it; for we are well able to overcome it." As daring as his conviction was firm, his assurance of faith impelled a verdict of obedience. Caleb saw everything in relationship to God, to His will and power.

Caleb lived through the 40 years of frustration and futility in the wilderness wanderings. In what possible way did he see it significant to follow God in this barren wilderness? Why not just resign himself that he, too, soon would die? "After all," he might have said, "I'm getting up in years. Shouldn't I just quietly back off? I'm well past retirement age now. This is a good time to call it quits. There's really nothing I need to do." (*"Need* to do?" What about *challenged* to do? *commanded* to do?) Caleb's best years were

just ahead. By the anticipation of faith, he was already living in that land of God's promise.

When the 40 years of wandering had ended, Caleb was
85 years old. What about you, older retiree? Are you going
to be like Caleb, ever learning the things of God, ever growing in trust and commitment? There are battles to fight, for
instance, to live triumphantly through a debilitating illness
with joy filling the heart and a word of rejoicing and praise
on the lips. Acceptance of illness as God's plan is your
choice as victor. But whatever size the obstacles, God will
give the strength to conquer, and you'll be glad through all
eternity you did!

Amazingly Caleb faced the most dreaded of the enemies awaiting Israel's troops—the fearful giants of Anakim.
He didn't opt for a lesser task. He said, "If so be the LORD
will be with me, then I shall be able to drive them out"
(Josh. 14:12, KJV). Note: "the LORD . . . with me . . . I
shall." Valiantly, Caleb drove them out!

At whatever age, obstacles threaten our progress to realize life in Christ. But God puts them there to purify our
lives and to conform us to His own character! These are the
very conditions of achievement, the very means toward developing the graces and virtues that we yearn and pray for.

It might well be that had Caleb's eyes been on his own
resources, a faint heart would have overcome him. To look
at such circumstances would cause any man among them
to resign himself to total defeat. But Caleb's gaze was fixed
on God who was as good as His promise.

Success may be living a faithful, joyous witness in a retirement home—to God a significant mountain. Or it may
be years of doing the impossible in the strength of Him
who is God of the impossible. Life need not become nar-
rower just because challenges become fewer.

A further note to you who are at the point of "compulsory inactivity." As God's child you still may pray for mission endeavors around the world as an intercessor before the throne of God. You may be an encourager of all those who are sent your way. Amy Carmichael, who has blessed thousands with her inspiring writing, did so as she lay in bed through the years that followed a fall from which she never recovered and that never permitted her to be about her mission work.

Listen to Scripture:

"The LORD is my strength" (Exod. 15:2, NKJV).

"Your God has commanded your strength; strengthen, O God, what you have done for us" (Ps. 68:28, NKJV).

"Not that we are adequate in ourselves . . . but our adequacy is from God" (2 Cor. 3:5, NASB).

The influence of mature Christians is desperately needed to help stabilize the church in this postmodern world. The younger need the older and wiser, the older need the younger with their vision and energy. We need to remember: the young are busy grasping the future while the older are busy conserving the past.

Caleb's example urges us not to settle for a useless retirement. Like Caleb, it should be said of us that we "wholly followed the LORD." Whatever God calls us to do, wherever He leads, it's our privilege and duty to do as Caleb, to wholly follow Him. Commit yourself once again to do just this.

7

Keeping Eternity's Values in View

What comes from man will never last,
It's here today, tomorrow past;
What comes from God will always be
The same for all eternity!

—Spencer

As I look over the length and events of my own life, I realize important questions I had to deal with: "What is now the deepest longing of my heart? Is it a longing satisfied by anything this life can bring? How am I compelled to look beyond retirement itself, so that the purposes I'm pursuing presently bring spiritual reassurance, making this stage of life fully satisfying and meaningful?"

A book I found helpful during my recovery from depressive crisis was Peter Kreeft's *Heaven: The Heart's Deepest Longing.*

We've been tracing the last stage of life when, having laid down his or her life-work, a person is faced with such fundamental questions as, "How shall my final years be lived meaningfully in terms of God's claim upon my life? As the years shorten and losses surpass gains, how shall I live with eternity's values in view? How can I prepare for the final great transition from earth to heaven?"

What better time than these less-harried years to contemplate the whole of our life's meaning, making the approaching end an integral part of one's overall valuation. Has the heart's deepest longing been left unrecognized amid the scramble to find substitute satisfactions, or perhaps buried in the subconscious altogether? Is this longing something only briefly and superficially pondered but never in depth? John writes that we "[have] eternal life"—present tense (3:36). Inasmuch as we now possess eternal life, all that remains is our change in location and transformation into our Lord's likeness. In a very practical sense, we are to live the eternal life we already possess.

Kreeft takes a clue from Malcolm Muggeridge who declared he found his chief blessing in his deepest sorrow. Muggeridge speaks of our being strangers in a strange land—displaced persons in this world, and he calls this "the greatest of all blessings." How is this? He describes it as follows: "The only ultimate disaster that can befall us, I have come to realize, is to feel ourselves to be at home here on earth. As long as we are aliens, we cannot forget our true homeland."[1]

Kreeft continues: "What is that longing? It is the greatest thing on earth because it leads us to heaven, which is the greatest thing of all. Earthly dissatisfaction is the road to heavenly satisfaction."[2]

Being dissatisfied may eventually bring about our greatest satisfaction—attainment of our true homeland. This answer is supported by the famous declaration of Augustine in his *Confessions*: "Thou hast made us for thyself and our hearts are restless until they rest in thee." Centuries of Christian thought affirm that the way to true rest is first "restlessness" with the present life. That restlessness causes us to long for a transformation that can bring to our spirits true and lasting rest. This rest is found chiefly in God but includes the place He has prepared for us—*heaven*, our ultimate and abiding home.

How often a suite of rooms in a retirement center—
where some readers are presently living—is something far
less than what was enjoyed over the years. Retirees settle
for a compromise, resigning themselves to this last "home."
They accept smaller quarters—excellent for some but for
others a source of dissatisfaction. Although easier to manage and get around, it does not have enough room for
keeping cherished possessions. A necessary compromise at
best. It is a home, but not *our home.*

Jesus assured us, "I go to prepare a place for you." How
wonderful indeed! But that place is not something we can see
or experience except through eyes of faith. When at last we
are in our heavenly home, we shall know it to be our true
home. Until then we have only the promise of the place prepared. It recalls that marvelous hymn titled "Finally Home."

Kreeft continues: Not only do we rest in God, he says;
"Heaven is home . . . our place." C. S. Lewis wrote: "Your
place in heaven will seem to be made for you and you
alone, because you were made for it."[3] Kreeft adds: "It is
our home because we receive there our true identity. We
don't know who we are, remember; we are alienated not
only from our home but from our selves."[4]

How very true! Our identity is that of a child of God living in a sinful world, struggling to maintain our separation
from that which is of the world, often having mixed feelings about our true identity. But in heaven we shall know
our true selves in Christ. And we shall glory in knowing
our loved ones as true selves in Christ.

This matter of elusive, ever-changing personal identity
can get confused in the transitions of life. Strangely com-
forting is our knowledge that all our human brothers and
sisters—all humanity—lost their true identity in Eden, but
that lost Eden was not intended to be our abiding home.
That home is heaven. There our identity will be restored,

and we shall be glorified, made complete in our Savior's image! We will reflect Him in His perfection! In his Gospel, John said we shall be with Him, in his first Epistle we shall be like Him. What completeness is ours in Christ—"conformed to the image of his Son" (Rom. 8:29)! Can we even begin to imagine this?

Kreeft gives us this important word: "The experience of longing for the past that is unattainably gone is our deep nostalgia brought about by the knowledge of death. It is seeing our past with the eyes of death before we die."[5]

Unless heaven is part of our overall perspective in retirement, we miss retirement's most precious prospect. Time then becomes our enemy. Aging takes the form of an uncertain and foreboding prospect. C. S. Lewis wrote two letters to Sheldon Vanauken in which he discusses the death of his (Lewis's) wife, Joy. He states at length the fact that time and death are both our enemy and friend, describing time as a slippery slope toward death and further commenting that it is simply another name for death. Yet, he continues, time and death are also friends for the reason that, in a final sense, they are what frame our lives. Indeed, with Lewis we realize that the sense of the preciousness of life is heightened when we acknowledge that our lives are short and that we are soon to die. Life and death—every retiree's ultimate considerations.

In these final fleeting years of retirement our lives ought to be more precious, not less! We stand on this shore, looking toward the fulfillment of life on a distant shore. In the skies we see the glow of a beautiful sunset beckoning us on!

Country of Exile

Earlier we discussed the nature of time and its meaning to those who are feeling squeezed by time's relentless onward march. Once again we face the inevitable reality of death.

The crux of it all is expressed in Kreeft's question, "Time is our country of exile; how do we get home to eternity?"[6]

Without the assurance of an eternal home, our time on earth—when weeks and months are racing by—is little more than occupying a country of exile, with all the forebodings an exile represents to the human spirit. As C. S. Lewis says, "Time is just another name for death." Does that sound morbid? It shouldn't. Death is integral with life and for the Christian is birth into the new life in Christ—the fullness of life in Him!

Is this not the issue that presses upon the mind of every thoughtful Christian retiree? Don't you love Kreeft's two expressions "exiles from Eden" and "apprentices to heaven"? Scripture itself uses the terms "exiles" and "pilgrims."

We have a true nostalgia for that which was lost in Eden, centered as it was in the bliss of knowing the intimate presence of God. It is nostalgia that looks back to Eden but only in order to look ahead to heaven.

We are to be like Moses of whom it was said in what we know as the faith chapter, "he endured as seeing him who is invisible" (Heb. 11:27). The writer of Hebrews tells of the Israelites acknowledging that they were but strangers and exiles on the earth, adding, "For here we have no lasting city, but we seek the city which is to come" (13:14). The older we grow the more we recognize we do not have a lasting city or home. There are no life situations in which to take final refuge, no place of ultimate personal fulfillment. We are pilgrims proceeding along on a swiftly passing tide. Time is the river that sweeps us away. *We ought to be homesick for heaven!*

Earth Haunted by Heaven

Early on, Kreeft introduces the notion of "Earth haunted by Heaven," a complex notion.[7] In it he notes that "the world we see is haunted by something we do not see—an unseen presence. . . . It seems to come from another dimension, another kind of reality than the world it haunts."[8]

The haunting leads us to expect to see the invisible, to know the unknowable—the very reality of God's presence. Our minds and vision will be so transformed as to see and know reality as it truly is. The unreality we see in this life is like a kaleidoscope where everything changes and nothing is constant.

Kreeft introduces a superb, if unexpected, illustration—*romantic love:*

> The transcendent longing that inspired the romantic lover to jettison all prudence and calculation for the ecstasy of union with the beloved is always in the long run disappointed by that union. . . . It always promises more than it can possibly deliver. It promises ecstasy; it delivers only intense pleasure. It promises . . . a self-transcendence . . . a mystical transformation. But it delivers only a tiny intimation of this at best, which only whets the appetite for the real thing . . . Once the beauty of the beloved is grasped, it disappears.[9]

The theme of romantic love is one to which I devoted two chapters in my book *How Should I Love You?*[10] Kreeft's analysis is right on target. He then asks the logical question:

"Why do we keep repeating the mistake? Why do many people go through an endless succession of earthly loves (persons, things) even after repeated experience tells them they are always disappointed?"[11]

We might specify Kreeft's "earthly loves" as material possessions, sexual fulfillment, recognition of achievements. To his own question, Kreeft replies that we continue trying in spite of repeated failures because we're actually looking for God—but in all the wrong places. Indeed we are!

Pascal put it somewhat differently in his observation that "the infinite abyss" (our passionate desire for things of earth) "can be filled only with an infinite and immutable object, in other words with God himself."[12] Pascal spoke, you recall, of that God-formed vacuum in the soul of every person. In every age, the human race has proved the truth of this observation.

Returning Exiles

Is it any wonder that throughout life we search for things that are immutable, things that eventually will prove not to be transient in their ability to satisfy? Yet we always search in vain. All earthly joys—none excepted—are transient. Nothing of earth can truly satisfy the longing heart, only God himself.

How, then, shall we know Him, the Living God? It is through a personal faith-relationship with His Son, the Lord Jesus Christ, that we know God personally as the Eternal Father. By faith, we are one with Him. As nothing less than God himself can satisfy the human soul, and since the Lord Jesus himself is the revelation of the Father, He is rightfully the object of every longing heart.

We who trust the Savior are "heirs of God and fellow heirs with Christ" (Rom. 8:17). If heirs, then, of course, we have an inheritance. Peter speaks of "an inheritance which is imperishable, undefiled, unfading, kept in heaven for you, who by God's power are guarded through faith for a salvation ready to be revealed in the last time" (1 Pet. 1:4). Heb. 9:15 calls it "the promised eternal inheritance."

We know something extraordinarily substantial about heaven inasmuch as we know the Lord of heaven. He said He was going to prepare a place for us and that He would come and take us unto himself that where He is we shall be also (John 14:3). Yes, heaven is home—*our home, our home with Jesus, our home with loved ones!*

An Exquisite Argument

There is the well-known argument of C. S. Lewis, which Kreeft calls "the single most intriguing argument in the history of human thought." The following is based on portions of Lewis's argument.[13]

Lewis's major premise is that every true innate desire we have has a corresponding reality that satisfies that desire. His minor premise is that there exists in us a desire that nothing can satisfy whether on earth or in time. Therefore, that which correspondingly satisfies this inherent, God-placed desire must exist outside of earth and time. Is not "the Person" God himself? And "the place" heaven itself?

This twin truth is brought together in Jesus' promise to the disciples in two different passages. First, John 14:3, "that where I am you may be also." For the Christian, the "Person" and "place" combine, for John also declared that "we shall be like him, for we shall see him as he is" (1 John 3:2).

Where does this longing reside and from whence does it arise? It comes from within ourselves; it is not imported from anywhere outside ourselves save that it is God who places it within us. Moreover, this is the one genuinely imperious desire to spring from within us, proof of what to us is presently unknown, undefinable, without representation in the world of our experience. Nonetheless, that desire indicates the very presence of a corresponding reality, infinitely more than any human representation could make it. *God and heaven are the great realities!*

Insofar as eternal things can be revealed, and insofar as the infinite can be depicted to finite minds, God has given us hints. And so far as the deepest longing of the heart is concerned, the writer of Ecclesiastes says, "He has put eternity into man's mind, yet so that he cannot find out what God has done from the beginning to the end" (3:11).

Description of heavenly things belongs to the vocabulary of heaven, not earth. What we recognize is that *this* is the haunting and *we* are the haunted. It is God himself who corresponds to that for which the heart longs in its haunting.

The Future Encounter

God reveals that the perfect knowledge of himself shall come through a future encounter. At that time, we shall be prepared to meet Him. Lewis places this overarching desire against all other desires—"an unsatisfied desire that is more desirable than any other satisfaction."

He continues: "Most people, if they had really learned to look into their own hearts, would know that they do want, and want acutely, something that cannot be had in this world. There are all sorts of things in this world that offer to give it to you, but they never quite keep their promise."[14]

The crux of the argument is, "If I find in myself a desire which no experience in this world can satisfy, the most probable explanation is that I was made for another world."[15]

So Lewis forcefully continues: "It appeared to me therefore that if a man diligently followed this desire, pursuing the false objects until their falsity appeared and then resolutely abandoning them, he must come out at last into the clear knowledge that the human soul is made to enjoy some object that is never fully given—nay, cannot even be imagined as given—in our present mode of subjective and spatio-temporal experience."[16]

Restless Until We Rest in Him

Lewis's argument speaks to the restlessness we all know, the restlessness that becomes acute and painful to the Christian retiree who has laid down his career, taken on a pattern of life with unbearable amounts of leisure time to fill, and who desperately wants to know the meaning of his earthly life in its entire course right to the appointed end. No greater question confronts him than "How can I live before God so as to prepare myself to see His face in the near future? How can I live with eternity's values in view? Until that time, how can my life be lived significantly for God?"

As in all things human, there is a dark side that must not be overlooked. It has been called the residual inner contradiction, and it is an acknowledgment of the unredeemed elements continuing within us. The apostle Paul speaks of this in Gal. 5, especially in verse 17. Following an admonition to walk by the Spirit and not gratify the desires of the flesh, he points to the flesh/spirit dichotomy that characterizes every genuine believer until the time of his or her arrival in heaven. Paul says, "The flesh sets its desire against the Spirit, and the Spirit against the flesh; for these are in opposition to one another, so that you may not do the things that you please" (Gal. 5:17, NASB).

How does this inner residual pull toward the things of earth affect our longing for heaven? That longing is in fine balance—the natural fear of things unknown against the human proclivity to cling to that which is known. It is the familiar striving against the unfamiliar. As a pastor friend, Arvid Carlson, said to me in a conversation about our departure to be with the Lord, "What a wonderful prospect—yet how *awesome*" Indeed it is! While we do not fear death itself, or have anxiety about the means of our entrance into heaven, we have a natural apprehension about things unfamiliar, not easily removed even by faith. Add to *"awesome"* the word *"glorious."*

The writer of the Book of Hebrews speaks of those "who through fear of death were subject to lifelong bondage" (2:15). In Christian hearts this fear, this very real bondage, no longer remains, only the overpowering awesomeness of the unfamiliar. The reason for this correlates with our previous discussion of why we have a tendency to look back. We cannot identify ourselves within the history of eternity, or yet within the environs of heaven. We *see* none of these things nor can we *experience* them now. Just as the future here is not mapped out to our minds, so heaven is not mapped out to our eyes. This grappling with ultimate reality is likely to be enhanced as we approach the end of our days. For these things are received by faith, not by explanation. Still, God has a word for this time:

"Be anxious for nothing, but in everything by prayer and supplication, with thanksgiving, let your requests be made known to God; and the peace of God, which surpasses all understanding, will guard your hearts and minds through Christ Jesus" (Phil. 4:6-7, NKJV).

Even when we no longer look to things earthly for our deepest satisfactions or our true identity, the residual pull nevertheless is great and is set against the reality of heaven's true bliss. Our victory, once more, comes as we continue in God's Word, in the strivings of prayer, and in a constantly renewed surrender to the Spirit's control.

The apostle further enables our understanding through his word to the Corinthians: "'What no eye has seen, nor ear heard, nor the heart of man conceived, what God has prepared for those who love him,' God has revealed to us through the Spirit" (1 Cor. 2:9-10).

This is followed by a word of assurance that we who are in Christ are not left on our own in this life but have the Spirit and His ministry enabling our understanding. We are strengthened for the battle against the "residual inner contradiction" of our fleshly life.

Concluding Personal Note

Hannah Whitall Smith first published her classic *The Christian's Secret of a Happy Life* in 1875. Literally millions have been taught and blessed in the century and a quarter following publication. I was blessed in reading this book just months after my conversion at age 14, and now again many years later. Toward the close of her life, she wrote her spiritual autobiography. The final chapter begins, "And now that I am seventy years old . . ." But, wait, before I quote her, let me insert this personal note.

I quote her words because they reflect my own story at the present time. I, too, am now in my later years. Insofar as active service roles are concerned, my retirement years remain somewhat uncertain healthwise. I have learned through my own retirement identity crisis, along with the uncertainty of long-standing diabetic health problems, to rest in His appointments day by day. As the issue was posed earlier, the question is not what we *do* with whatever time He allots, so much as with what we *are*—or more precisely—*what we are becoming* in the love and grace of our God and our Savior. It is the maturing life in Christ that matters most, and to me is most important now—where my own life gladly centers. And should you the reader find that aging or health no longer allows you to be an active servant of God, listen to Hannah Whitall Smith:

> To be seventy gives one permission to stand aloof from the stress of life, and to lay down all burden of re-sponsibility for carrying on the work of the world; and I rejoice in my immunity. . . . I am more than happy to

know that the responsibilities of the present generation do not rest upon me, but upon the shoulders of the younger and stronger spirits, who are called in the providence of God to bear them. I laugh to myself with pleasure at the thought, and quite enjoy the infirmities of age as they come upon me, and find it delightful to be laid aside from one thing after another, and to be at liberty to look on in a peaceful leisure at the younger wrestlers in the world's arena. I cannot say that their wrestling is always done in the way that seems best to my old eyes, but I admire the Divine order that evidently lays upon each generation its own work, to be done in its own way; and I am convinced that, whether it may seem to us for good or for ill, the generation that is passing must give place to the one that is coming, and must keep hands off from interfering. Advice we who are old may give, and the fruits of our experience, but we must be perfectly content to have our advice rejected by the younger generation, and our experience ignored.[17]

Note that Hannah Whitall Smith does not sigh with regret when she says, "To be seventy . . ." She is glad to pass the torch to those who follow. There comes the time when we need to do the same—and without regrets.

Former U.S. President Jimmy Carter, in his book *The Virtues of Aging*, says, "It is better to be seventy years young than forty years old!"[18] That's the spirit! What an antidote for the person laid aside for whatever reason, be it age, health, or lack of opportunity! How easy to feel that we must be in the thick of the battle until the end, that we must not miss God's design for the seasons of life even as this season is shutting down. What we need in our closing years is fresh realization of the restfulness of contemplating God and all His works. Retirement, whatever active role it does or does not afford us individually, is the time to meditate deeply on the glories of the life ahead. May preparing for "going home" determine everything that occupies us in these closing bonus years.

My good friend Donald Barnhouse Jr. offers this excellent word:

> History and time are nothing more than the framework within which God is trying to win back our trust. When limits go, they will go. Life is a big word, but life now is only a shadow of what it is intended to be. Death is the last enemy, and it will be destroyed. In the meanwhile, until that is accomplished, death will be made to serve throughout history as the gate by which we pass from this damaged life into a new and perfect life. For those who trust God, this gate has the marvelous property as you get closer to it of looking less like an exit and more and more like an entrance.[19]

This brings us to that distinctly Christian word—*hope.* Of the three things Paul calls the greatest in 1 Cor. 13, along with such mighty attributes as *faith* and *love* comes *hope.* The Christian life matures on hope. Faith engenders hope— hope for the present wherever the "present" happens to find us, hope for the future of our days however long or short that future may appear, and best of all, hope for that day when we arrive on heaven's shore. As for now, faith and hope grasp life as it is, looking beyond to see what otherwise is unknown. We can live in hope whatever our circumstances may be.

Several years ago, millionaire Eugene Lang was asked to speak to a class of sixth-graders in a poor East Harlem, New York, school. In their presence, he was inspired to scrap his speech and spoke from his heart about staying in school, adding, "I'll help pay the college tuitions for every one of you."

For those students this was a turning point from hopelessness to hope. Nearly 90 percent of that class went on to graduate from high school, many going on to college. Bill Gates and others have taken up the same challenge in our day.

Roy Fairchild, in his book *Finding Hope Again*, reminds us that hope is not mere optimism, nor is it "positive thinking." Positive thinking does not engender hope; rather, hope engenders positive thinking. The person of hope so often finds that hope is generated out of a tragic sense of life, becoming a window looking out on brighter possibilities, enlarging the significance of the present, for it is alive with potential.[20] Hope enables retirees to grasp the unknown with full assurance that God is in it all—*and for our good!*

What brings this all together? J. Sidlow Baxter, friend of many years and beloved Bible teacher, in his book *Does God Still Guide?* gives us these lines:

Lord, help me clearly understand,
My way is all by Thee foreplanned;
And I, full yielding to Thy will,
Life's richest purpose may fulfill.

With each new winding of the way,
New guidance may be mine each day;
A yielded heart in daily prayer
Discerns Thy watch-care everywhere.

Each day, as I with Thee commune,
Lord, set my heart and mind attune,
To hear the inward Voice divine,
With scarce a need for outward sign.

So, guided through my earthly days,
Safeguarded thus from error's maze,
My heav'nward pilgrimage shall be
A deepening fellowship with Thee."[21]

We have the assuring words in Phil. 2:13: "God is at work in you, both to will and to work for his good pleasure." This leads to a most appropriate benediction in the words of Heb. 13:20-21: "Now may the God of peace . . . equip you with everything good that you may do his will, working in you that which is pleasing in his sight."

Let's conclude with a minute of inspiration from lines taken from the following three stanzas in the hymn by B. Mansell Ramsey titled "Teach Me Thy Way, O Lord."

> *Long as my life shall last,*
> *Teach me Thy way!*
> *Where'er my lot be cast,*
> *Teach me Thy way!*
> *Until the race is run,*
> *Until the journey's done,*
> *Until the crown is won,*
> *Teach me Thy way!*

Agnes Maude Royden said, "Hold loosely all that is not eternal."[22]

Notes

Introduction

1. Alex Comfort, *A Good Age* (New York: Crown Publishers, 1976), 182.

2. Page Smith, *Old Age Is Another Country: A Traveler's Guide* (Freedom, Calif.: The Crossing Press, 1995), 172.

Chapter 1

1. William Bridges, *Transitions: Making Sense of Life's Changes* (Menlo Park, Calif.: Addison-Wesley Publishing Company, 1980), 52.

2. Jules Z. Willing, *The Reality of Retirement* (New York: William Morrow and Company, 1981), 30.

3. Ibid.

4. John Oxenham, *Selected Poems of John Oxenham* (London: Adelphi/T. Fisher Unwin, Ltd., 1924), 52.

Chapter 2

1. Timothy K. Jones, "Reading Life Backwards," *Christianity Today,* September 22, 1989, 28.

2. Ibid., 31.

3. Simone de Beauvoir, *The Coming of Age* (New York: G. P. Putnam's Sons, 1972), 372.

4. Lloyd John Ogilvie, *Silent Strength for My Life* (Eugene, Oreg.: Harvest House Publishers, 1990), 122.

5. John Baillie, *A Diary of Private Prayer* (New York: Charles Scribner's Sons, 1949), 115.

Chapter 3

1. Judith Viorst, *Necessary Losses* (New York: Simon and Schuster, 1986), 290.

2. Ibid., 237.

3. Ibid., 325-26.

4. John W. James and Frank Cherry, *The Grief Recovery Handbook* (New York: Harper and Row Publishing, 1988), 4.

5. Ibid., 13.

6. Viorst, *Necessary Losses,* 249.

7. Quoted in C. S. Lewis, *A Grief Observed* (Greenwich, Conn.: Seabury Press, 1963), 39.

8. Ibid., 247.

9. Viorst, *Necessary Losses,* 264.

10. John Bowlby, *Attachment and Loss,* vol. 3 (New York: Basic Books, Inc., 1980), 174.

11. Archibald D. Hart, *Feeling Free* (Old Tappan, N.J.: Fleming H. Revell Company, 1979), 101 ff.

Chapter 4

1. R. Butler, "The Life Review: An Interpretation of Reminiscence in the Aged," *Psychiatry* 26 (1963): 65-76; C. S. Lewis, "Reminiscence and Self-Concept in Old Age," *Journal of Gerontology* 26, No. 2 (1971): 240-43; Marcel Proust, *The Past Recaptured* (New York: Albert and Charles Boni, 1932).

2. Peter Kreeft, *Heaven: The Heart's Deepest Longing* (San Francisco: Ignatius Press, 1989), 75.

3. Willing, *Reality of Retirement,* 30.

4. Jones, *Christianity Today,* 28-33.

5. Lee Butcher, *Retirement Without Fear* (Princeton, N.J.: Dow Jones Books, 1978).

Chapter 5

1. Paul Tournier, *Learn to Grow Old* (New York: Harper and Row Publishing, 1971), 28. (See excellent research on this subject: Betty Friedan, *The Fountain of Age* [New York, Simon and Schuster, 1993].)

2. Roger L. Gould, *Transformations: Growth and Change in Adult Life* (New York: Simon and Schuster, 1978), 318.

3. Tournier, *Learn to Grow Old,* 142.

4. Ibid., 143.

5. Nikos Kazantzakis, *Zorba the Greek* (New York: Ballantine Books, by arrangement with Simon and Schuster, 1964), 138-39.

6. Ibid., 139.

7. Gabriel Rudney, "A Quantitative Profile of the Independent Sector," *Working Paper,* No. 40 (Program on Non-Profit Organizations, Institutions for Social and Policy Studies, Yale University, 1981), 3.

Chapter 6

1. Tournier, *Learn to Grow Old,* 169.

2. Gould, *Transformations,* 231.

3. Viktor E. Frankl, *Man's Search for Meaning* (New York: Washington Square Press, 1963).

4. E. Stanley Jones, *The Divine Yes* (Nashville: Abingdon Press, 1975).

5. Ibid., 85.

6. Michael Cassidy, *The Passing Summer* (Ventura, Calif.: Regal Books, 1989), 147.

7. Ibid., 472.

Chapter 7

1. Malcolm Muggeridge, *Jesus Rediscovered* (New York: Doubleday, 1979), 47-48.

2. Kreeft, *Heaven,* 63.

3. C. S. Lewis, *The Problem of Pain* (New York: Macmillan Publishing Company, 1962), 147-48.

4. Kreeft, *Heaven,* 67.

5. Ibid.

6. Ibid., 97.

7. Ibid., 104.

8. Ibid., chapter 3.

9. Ibid., 105.

10. Dwight Hervey Small, *How Should I Love You?* (San Francisco: Harper and Row Publishing, 1979).

11. Kreeft, *Heaven,* 105.

12. Blaise Pascal, *Pensees* (New York: Penguin Books, 1960), 120.

13. C. S. Lewis, *Mere Christianity* (New York: Macmillan, 1960), 130-31.

14. Ibid., 120.

15. Ibid.

16. Quoted in Kreeft, *Heaven,* 207.

17. Hannah Whitall Smith, *The Unselfishness of God* (Princeton, N.J.: Littlebrook Publishing, Inc., 1987), 229-30.

18. Jimmy Carter, *The Virtues of Aging* (New York: Ballantine Books, 1998), 109. This book is highly recommended and adds to themes in our study.

19. Donald Barnhouse Jr., *Is Anybody Up There?* (New York: Seabury Press, 1977), 122.

20. Roy W. Fairchild, *Finding Hope Again: A Pastor's Guide to Counseling Depressed Persons* (San Francisco: Harper and Row, Publishers, 1980).

21. J. Sidlow Baxter, *Does God Still Guide?* (Grand Rapids: Zonder-van Publishing House, 1971), 84.

22. Quoted in A. W. Tozer, *The Pursuit of God,* comp. Edythe Draper (Camp Hill, Pa.: Christian Publications, 1995), 21.

Select
Bibliography

Ahlem, Lloyd H. *Living and Growing in Later Years.* Chicago: Evangelical Covenant Church in America, 1992.

Baillie, John. *A Diary of Private Prayer.* New York: Charles Scribner's Sons, 1949.

Baxter, J. Sidlow. *Does God Still Guide?* Grand Rapids: Zondervan Publishing House, 1971.

Beauvoir, Simone de. *The Coming of Age.* New York: G. P. Putnam's Sons, 1972.

Bennett, William J. *The Book of Virtues.* New York: Simon & Schuster, 1993.

Bowlby, John. *Attachment and Loss.* Vol. 3. New York: Basic Books, 1980.

Bridges, William. *Transitions: Making Sense of Life's Changes.* Menlo Park, Calif.: Addison-Wesley Publishing Company, 1980.

Buford, Bob. *Game Plan: Winning Strategies for the Second Half.* Grand Rapids: Zondervan Publishing House, 1997.

———. *Half Time: Changing Your Game Plan from Success to Significance.* Grand Rapids: Zondervan Publishing House, 1997.

Butcher, Lee. *Retirement Without Fear.* Princeton, N.J.: Dow Jones Books, 1978.

Butler, R. "The Life Review: An Interpretation of Reminiscence in the Aged." *Psychiatry* 26 (1963), 65-76.

Carter, Jimmy. *The Virtues of Aging.* New York: The Library of Contemporary Thought, Ballantine Publishing Group, 1998.

Comfort, Alex. *A Good Age.* New York: Crown Publishing, 1976.

Fairchild, Roy W. *Finding Hope Again: A Pastor's Guide to Counseling Depressed Persons.* San Francisco: Harper & Row, 1980.

Frankl, Viktor E. *Man's Search for Meaning.* New York: Washington Square Press, 1963.

French, Virginia R. *Avoiding the Retirement Trap: Fifty Profiles of People Doing Something Meaningful with Their Retirement.* Chicago: ACTA Publishing, 1994.

Frieden, Betty. *The Fountain of Age.* New York: Simon and Schuster, 1993.

Fyock, Catherine D., and Anne M. Docton. *Un-Retirement: A Career Guide for the Retired . . . the Soon-to-Be Retired . . . the Never-Want-to-Be-Retired.* New York: AMACOM, 1994.

Gould, Roger. *Transformations: Growth and Change in Adult Life.* New York: Simon and Schuster, 1978.

Gubrium, Jaber F., ed. *Time, Roles and Self in Old Age.* New York: Human Science Press, 1976.

Hart, Archibald D. *Feeling Free.* Old Tappan, N.J.: Fleming H. Revell, 1979.

Hayford, Jack. *Taking Hold of Tomorrow.* Ventura, Calif.: Regal Books, 1989.

James, John W., and Frank Cherry. *The Grief Recovery Handbook.* New York: Harper and Row, 1988.

Jones, E. Stanley. *The Divine Yes.* Nashville: Abingdon Press, 1975.

Kreeft, Peter. *Heaven: The Heart's Deepest Longing.* San Francisco: Ignatius Press, 1989.

Langer, Ellen, et al. *Higher Stages of Human Development.* Ed. Charles Alexander and Ellen Langer. New York: Oxford University Press, 1987.

Lewis, C. S. *A Grief Observed.* Greenwich, Conn.: Seabury Press, 1963.

———. "Reminiscence and Self-Concept in Old Age." *Journal of Gerontology* 26 (1971): 2, 240-43.

Ogilvie, Lloyd John. *Silent Strength for My Life.* Eugene, Oreg.: Harvest House, 1990.

Prentis, Richard S. *Passages of Retirement: Personal Histories of Struggle and Success.* (Contributions to the Study of Aging series.) Belmont, Calif.: Greenwood Press, 1992.

Proust, Marcel. *The Past Recaptured.* New York: Albert and Charles Boni, 1932.

Publications from The Institute on Religion and Aging, 1100 W. 42nd St., Indianapolis, IN 46208.

Sayler, Mary H. *First Days of Retirement: Devotions to Begin Your Best Years.* Nashville: Broadman Press, 1995.

Sheehy, Gail. *New Passages.* New York: Random House, 1995.

Smith, Hannah Whitall. *The Unselfishness of God.* Princeton, N.J.: Littlebrook, 1987.

Smith, Page. *Old Age Is Another Country: A Traveler's Guide*. Freedom, Calif.: The Crossing Press, 1995.

"Successful Retirement" (No. 830) and "Think of Your Future: Pre-Retirement Planning" (No. 826). Booklets by the American Association of Retired Persons, 1865 Miner St., Des Plaines, IL 60016.

Tournier, Paul. *Learn to Grow Old*. New York: Harper and Row, 1971.

Tozer, A. W. *The Pursuit of God*. Comp. Edythe Draper. Camp Hill, Pa.: Christian Publications, 1995.

Vanauken, Sheldon. *A Severe Mercy*. San Francisco: Harper and Row, 1977.

Viorst, Judith. *Necessary Losses*. New York: Simon and Schuster, 1986.

Webber, Ann. *Growing into Fullness: Enjoying Retirement and Old Age*. Grand Rapids: Zondervan Publishing House, 1987.

Willing, Jules Z. *The Reality of Retirement*. New York: William Morrow and Company, 1981.